My revision notes

Edexcel A–level History

CIVIL RIGHTS AND RACE RELATIONS IN THE USA

1850–2009

Vivienne Sanders

Series editor
Peter Callaghan

HODDER
EDUCATION
AN HACHETTE UK COMPANY

Acknowledgements

The Publishers would like to thank the following for permission to reproduce copyright material.

p.41 The publisher wishes to thank the Crisis Publishing Co., Inc., the publisher of the magazine of the National Association for the Advancement of Colored People, for the use of this material first published in the October 1935 issue of Crisis Magazine.; p.44 The publisher wishes to thank the Crisis Publishing Co., Inc., the publisher of the magazine of the National Association for the Advancement of Colored People, for the use of this material first published in the August 1935 issue of Crisis Magazine.; p.51 Freedom Riders 40th Anniversary oral history project, Archives and Special collections, JD Williams library, The University of Mississippi.

Every effort has been made to trace all copyright holders, but if any have been inadvertently overlooked, the Publishers will be pleased to make the necessary arrangements at the first opportunity.

Although every effort has been made to ensure that website addresses are correct at time of going to press, Hodder Education cannot be held responsible for the content of any website mentioned in this book. It is sometimes possible to find a relocated web page by typing in the address of the home page for a website in the URL window of your browser.

Hachette UK's policy is to use papers that are natural, renewable and recyclable products and made from wood grown in sustainable forests. The logging and manufacturing processes are expected to conform to the environmental regulations of the country of origin.

Orders: please contact Bookpoint Ltd, 130 Milton Park, Abingdon, Oxon OX14 4SE. Telephone: +44 (0)1235 827720. Fax: +44 (0)1235 400401. Email: education@bookpoint.co.uk Lines are open from 9 a.m. to 5 p.m., Monday to Saturday, with a 24-hour message answering service. You can also order through our website: www.hoddereducation.co.uk

ISBN: 978 1 5104 1808 0

© Vivienne Sanders 2018
First published in 2018 by
Hodder Education,
An Hachette UK Company
Carmelite House
50 Victoria Embankment
London EC4Y 0DZ

www.hoddereducation.co.uk

Impression number 10 9 8 7 6 5 4 3 2 1

Year   2022 2021 2020 2019 2018

Cover photo © TopFoto.co.uk
Illustrations by Integra
Typeset by Integra Software Services Pvt. Ltd., Pondicherry, India
Printed in India

A catalogue record for this title is available from the British Library.

My Revision Planner

REVISED

Introduction

About Paper 3

Paper 3 Civil rights and race relations in the USA, 1850–2009 combines a depth study of emancipation and moves towards greater equality with a broader thematic study of changing perceptions of race relations, 1850–2009. Paper 3 tests you against two Assessment Objectives: AO1 and AO2:

AO1 tests your ability to:

- organise and communicate your own knowledge
- analyse and evaluate key features of the past
- make supported judgements
- deal with concepts of cause, consequence, change, continuity, similarity, difference and significance.

On Paper 1, AO1 tasks require you to write essays from your own knowledge.

AO2 tests your ability to:

- analyse and evaluate source material from the past
- explore the value of source material by considering its historical context.

On Paper 2, the AO2 task requires you to write an essay which analyses two sources which come from the period you have studied.

Paper 3 is worth 30 per cent of your A-level.

Structure

Paper 3 is structured around two themes and five key topics.

The exam is divided into three sections, which relate to different aspects of your course:

Aspect of the course	Exam
Topic 1: 'Free at last', 1865–77	Section A (AO2) and Section B (AO1)
Topic 2: The triumph of 'Jim Crow', 1883–c1900	
Topic 3: The New Deal and race relations, 1933–41	
Topic 4: 'I have a dream', 1954–68	
Topic 5: Obama's campaign for the presidency, 2004–09	
Theme 1: The changing geography of civil rights issues	Section C (AO1)
Theme 2: Changing portrayal of civil rights issues in fiction and film	

The exam

The Paper 3 exam lasts for 2 hours and 15 minutes, and is divided into three sections.

Section A and Section B test the depth of your historical knowledge of the five topics:

Section A requires you to answer one compulsory question concerning a single Source. You should spend 15 to 20 minutes reading the Source and planning your answer, and around 35 to 40 minutes writing the essay.

Section B requires you to write one essay from a choice of two. As this is a depth paper, questions can be set on single events. Section B essays usually tests your knowledge of a shorter period than Section C. You should spend 35 to 40 minutes on Section B.

Section C requires you to answer one question, from a choice of two. Questions in Section C will focus on the two themes. Questions will cover at least 100 years. Questions can focus on either themes, or may test knowledge of both themes. You should spend 35 to 40 minutes on Section C.

How to use this book

This book has been designed to help you to develop the knowledge and skills necessary to succeed in this exam. The book is divided into seven sections – one for each of the Aspects in Depth, and two for the Aspects in Breadth. Each section is made up of a series of topics organised into double-page spreads. On the left-hand page, you will find a summary of the key content you need to learn. Words in bold in the key content are defined in the Glossary. On the right-hand page, you will find exam-focused activities. Together, these two strands of the book will take you through the knowledge and skills essential for exam success.

There are three levels of exam focused activities.

- Band 1 activities are designed to develop the foundational skills needed to pass the exam.
- Band 2 activities are designed to build on the skills developed in Band 1 activities and to help you achieve a C grade.
- Band 3 activities are designed to enable you to access the highest grades.

Each section ends with an exam-style question and model high-level answer with commentary. This should give you guidance on what is required to achieve the top grades.

1 'Free at last', 1865–77

Reasons for, and importance of, the 13th Amendment (1865)

Background

Although the American Declaration of Independence (1776) said 'all men are created equal', most white Americans had considered black Americans inferior from the time slaves were first imported into America in the seventeenth century. The American **Constitution** (1787) accepted the existence of slavery, which further confirmed black inequality. White Southerners considered slavery essential because slaves seemed the ideal solution to the problem of the labour-intensive plantation agriculture that dominated the South.

Over 90 per cent of black Americans lived in the South and white Southerners feared that if they were freed they might prove hostile, compete for paid work, and threaten white racial purity and white supremacy.

As there were no plantations in the North, the Northern economy did not depend upon slaves, so by the early nineteenth century slavery had been abolished in most Northern states.

Northern and Southern disagreements over the continued expansion of slavery led to the American Civil War (1861–65), in which President **Abraham Lincoln's** Unionists (the North) eventually defeated the Confederates (the South).

During the Civil War, President Lincoln issued a preliminary Emancipation Proclamation (September 1862). It said:

- slavery could continue in states that returned to the Union before January 1863
- after that, all slaves in enemy territory conquered by Union armies would be free.

In January 1863, Lincoln proclaimed that the freedom of all slaves in enemy territory was now a Union war aim, 'an act of justice' as well as of 'military necessity'.

Lincoln issued the Emancipation Proclamation because:

- Union commanders needed clarification on the status of the 500,000 refugee slaves in Northern army camps
- the Union could use freed slaves and more slaves would be encouraged to flee and thereby weaken the Confederacy
- it might halt British aid to the Confederacy.

Reasons for the 13th Amendment

Congress approved the 13th **Amendment** during 1864–65, and by December 1865, sufficient states had ratified it.

There were several reasons for the 13th Amendment:

- Lincoln's Emancipation Proclamation (January 1863) did not end slavery throughout the United States, so abolitionists campaigned for a constitutional amendment to end slavery, e.g. the Women's National Loyal League's petition for an amendment had 500,000 signatures.
- Lincoln worried about the constitutional status of slavery, because the Constitution of 1787 recognised slavery and his Emancipation Proclamation was a war measure that might not be considered constitutional in peace time. A constitutional amendment was the most effective way to clarify the status of slavery.
- **Republicans** felt that slavery had caused terrible conflict and might do so again if retained.
- Many slaves had run away during the Civil War, so the restoration of slavery was impossible.
- Many Northerners recognised the freed slaves' contribution to the Union war effort and did not want to see them returned to slavery.

! Spot the mistake a

Below is a sample exam-style question and a paragraph written in answer to this question. Why would this paragraph not get high praise? What is wrong with the focus of the answer in this paragraph?

How far do you agree that the Civil War was a war fought to end slavery?

Before the Civil War, Lincoln said that although he did not want to see slavery spread westward, he did not seek to end slavery in the Southern states. In the years 1861–65, Lincoln's Northern states fought the slave-owning states of the Confederacy. The victory of the North owed much to the military brilliance of General Ulysses S. Grant and to Lincoln's political skills. In 1863, Lincoln issued the Emancipation Proclamation. This was a war measure rather than any reflection of any great Northern opposition to slavery. After the North defeated the South, the North's determination to end slavery was evident in the 13th Amendment (1865).

! Support or challenge? a

Below is a sample exam-style question which asks you to what extent you agree with a specific statement. Below that is a list of general statements which are relevant to the question. Using your own knowledge and the information on the opposite page, decide whether these statements support or challenge the statement in question.

How far do you agree that the main reason for the 13th Amendment was the abolitionists' campaign?

STATEMENT	SUPPORT	CHALLENGE
Lincoln was worried about the constitutional status of slaves.		
The Women's National Loyal League's petition gained 500,000 signatures.		
Slaves had run away during the Civil War.		
Republicans blamed slavery for the Civil War.		
The National Convention of Colored Men's meeting at Syracuse, New York, supported Lincoln for president and demanded black equality.		

The importance of the 13th Amendment (1865)

The 13th Amendment was extremely important in that it ended slavery, but also in that it did nothing to solve the problems of black economic, social and political inequality. Indeed, the 13th Amendment was important in that it generated acute social and political divisions.

The economic position of ex-slaves and the development of sharecropping

The 13th Amendment transformed the economy of the South. Without any slaves, plantation owners had to find workers and to pay them. Most freed slaves only knew how to farm, but they had no land. As a result, most freed slaves became sharecroppers (white landlords provided land and equipment, the sharecropper did the work, and both shared the crop profits). Sharecropping perpetuated black poverty and economic inequality. So, the 13th Amendment had ended slavery but had not solved the problem of black economic inequality.

Social tensions

The 13th Amendment generated social tensions. Southern whites were bitter at the loss of the war and resentful of freed blacks, particularly when they demanded greater equality. Much violence resulted when blacks demanded more rights and whites sought to maintain their racial supremacy, e.g. a Memphis mob killed over 40 black men in the race riots of the summer of 1866. So, the 13th Amendment had ended slavery, but had not solved the racial tensions that resulted from black freedom.

The need for a political settlement

The 13th Amendment and the freeing of the slaves raised the question of black political rights. White Southerners did not want blacks to be able to vote, but white Northerners were more sympathetic – especially Republicans, who knew that new black voters would vote Republican, the party of Abraham Lincoln. The 13th Amendment had helped create a great political problem.

President Andrew Johnson's response

After Lincoln's assassination (April 1865), Vice President **Andrew Johnson** became president. Johnson's greatest problem was what to do with the defeated South. The South's political, social and economic systems had been ruined and needed to be revived – this process is known as **Reconstruction**. Radical Republicans had been pleased with Johnson's wartime declaration that Confederates merited harsh punishments. However, as president, Johnson sided with the old Confederate elite because:

- he was a Southerner
- he wanted to ensure Southern white loyalty to the United States
- he believed in states' rights
- he considered black Americans inferior
- he thought the restoration of the old Confederate elite would assure his own re-election.

Johnson introduced what became known as 'Presidential Reconstruction'. He allowed any Southern state that accepted the end of slavery to return to the Union. Naturally, Southern whites reasserted their supremacy. One way in which they did this was through the introduction of 'Black Codes' that maintained black economic, social, political and legal inequality. Black Codes were designed to make it impossible for black Americans to

- purchase or rent land
- vote
- obtain an education
- receive meaningful protection from the law.

! Eliminate irrelevance — a

Below is a sample exam-style question and a paragraph written in answer to this question. Read the paragraph and identify parts of the paragraph that are not directly relevant to the question. Draw a line through the information that is irrelevant and justify your deletions in the margin.

How accurate is it to say that President Johnson's sympathy for the defeated white Southerners was unsurprising?

In some ways, Johnson's version of Reconstruction was a surprise. Radical Republicans had been impressed when the former slave-owner took a consistently tough wartime stance on the future of leading Confederates. In 1864, Johnson had said, 'Traitors must be punished and impoverished'. However, there are many factors that explain the sympathy Johnson demonstrated to the defeated Confederate elite during 1865. He was a typical Southerner. He had been born into poverty in North Carolina and had had a successful career as a tailor. Johnson shared the typical Southern white belief in black inequality. As politician and president, he wanted to ensure Southern white loyalty to the United States and to him — he thought the restoration of the old elite would help ensure his re-election. In the 1865 elections, the newly elected Southern congressmen included the Vice President of the Confederacy, 58 Confederate congressmen, and four Confederate generals. Finally, he was a firm believer in states' rights. For all these reasons, his sympathetic 'Presidential Reconstruction' was not surprising.

! Complete the paragraph — a

Below is a sample question and a paragraph written in answer to this question.

The paragraph contains a point and specific examples, but lacks a concluding analytical link back to the question. Complete the paragraph, adding this link back to the question in the space provided.

How far do you agree with Frederick Douglass's assertion that 'The work does not end with the abolition of slavery, but only begins'?

The abolition of slavery was essential if black Americans were to achieve equality. Without freedom of movement, slaves had lacked control over their own destiny. However, Douglass was right to suggest it was only a beginning, because freed slaves suffered economic, social and political inequality. They had no land and few marketable skills. Southern whites resented their defeat in the war and remained convinced of white supremacy. Former Confederates were also opposed to black Americans being given the vote. Overall, . . .

_____

_____

_____

Radical Reconstruction 1867–77, part 1

President Johnson had hoped to restore the South to the Union before Congress met in December 1865. However, Northern Republicans in the new Congress opposed his 'Presidential Reconstruction' and were resentful that the newly elected Southern representatives included the Vice President of the Confederacy, 58 Confederate congressmen, and four Confederate generals. The Republican majority

- refused to allow those members of the old Confederate elite to take their seats in the Congress
- refused to recognise the new Southern state governments (these were also dominated by the old Confederate elite)
- soon clashed with Johnson, e.g. over the 14th Amendment.

The 14th Amendment

The Republican-controlled Congress passed the 14th Amendment in 1866. The aim was to reinforce the 1866 **Civil Rights** Act. That Act and the 14th Amendment

- struck down the Black Codes
- guaranteed all citizens equality before the law
- allowed **federal government** intervention if any states denied citizens their rights
- banned most of the old Confederate elite from holding office.

However, the old Confederate states of the South refused to ratify the 14th Amendment.

By this time, Northerners were disgusted by a combination of

- the Southern states' rejection of the 14th Amendment
- the summer 1866 race riots in Southern cities, e.g. Memphis, New Orleans
- the growth of violent white supremacist organisations, e.g. the Ku Klux Klan (see page 14).

As a result, the Republican-dominated Congress decided to impose Congressional Reconstruction (aka 'Radical Reconstruction' or 'Black Reconstruction') on the South. This imposition was to be done through the provisions of the Military Reconstruction Act (1867).

The impact of military rule in the South

The Military Reconstruction Act had three main provisions:

1 It removed the old white Confederate elite from the US Congress and from state governments.

2 It said the Southern states could only return to the Union if they
- adopted constitutions that allowed black voting
- ratified the 14th Amendment
- forbade office-holding by former Confederate office holders.

3 It imposed government by military commanders upon the former Confederate states.

Military rule provoked different viewpoints. White Southerners and President Johnson considered it disastrous. They believed that the black population was given too much power under the military commanders. Black Southerners found military rule beneficial. It enabled them to vote and occupy public office, although it did not solve all the problems of inequality – especially economic inequality.

The 15th Amendment

Republicans (including **Ulysses S. Grant**, president in 1869–77) were keen to ensure that their party received the black vote in the South, so they promoted the 15th Amendment. The 15th Amendment said black Americans should have the vote, although it did not guarantee or safeguard that right. Black Americans in the South invariably voted Republican, because

- a Republican president had issued the Emancipation Proclamation
- a Republican-dominated Congress had supported the 14th and 15th Amendments and introduced the Military Reconstruction Act.

The 15th Amendment was ratified in 1870.

ⓘ Write the question   ⓐ

The following source relates to Radical Republican support for Congressional Reconstruction. Having read the material on the 14th and 15th Amendments, write an exam style question using the source. Remember, the question must focus on two enquiries.

Assess the value of the source for revealing

_____

and

_____

Explain your answer, using the source, the information given about its origin, and your own knowledge about the historical context.

SOURCE 1

From a speech in support of Congressional/Radical Reconstruction by Radical Republican leader Thaddeus Stevens in Congress, 3 January 1867.

Since the surrender of the armies of the Confederate States of America a little has been done toward establishing this Government upon the true principles of liberty and justice; and but a little if we stop here. We have broken the material shackles of four million slaves. We have unchained them from the stake so as to allow them locomotion, provided they do not walk in paths which are trod by white men. We have allowed them the unwonted privilege of attending church, if they can do so without offending the sight of their former masters. We have even given them that highest and most agreeable evidence of liberty as defined by the 'great plebeian' the 'right to work'. But in what have we enlarged their liberty of thought? In what have we taught them the science and granted them the privilege of self-government? We have imposed upon them the privilege of fighting battles, of dying in defence of freedom, and of bearing their equal portion of taxes, but where have we given them the privilege of ever participating in the formation of the laws for the government of their native land? By what civil weapon have we enabled them to defend themselves against oppression and injustice? Call you this liberty? Call you this a free Republic where four millions are subjects but not citizens? … Twenty years ago … twenty million white men enchained four million black men. I pronounce it no nearer to a true Republic now when twenty-five million of a privileged class exclude five million from all participation in the rights of government …

No Government can be free that does not allow all its citizens to participate in the formation and execution of her laws … Every man, no matter what his race or colour; every earthly being who has an immortal soul, has an equal right to justice, honesty, and fair play with every other man; and the law should secure those rights. The same law which condemns or acquits an African should condemn or acquit a white man … This doctrine does not mean that a negro shall sit on the same seat or eat at the same table as a white man.

The significance of the presence of black representation in federal and state legislatures

When black Southerners were given the vote, it enabled them to vote for candidates sympathetic for their needs – and particularly for black candidates. During Reconstruction, 700,000 black males were registered to vote in the South. They outnumbered the 600,000 white males (many old Confederates were disfranchised). These new black voters usually voted Republican.

Large-scale black voting had both positive and negative significance.

Positives

● Many black Americans were elected to federal and state offices in the South. This was a revolutionary advance.

● Between 1869 and 1877, 16 black congressmen and two black senators were elected to the US Congress, over 700 black males served in **state legislatures** and around 1,000 were elected to local posts such as sheriff.

● Black legislators naturally contributed to the passage of laws that helped black Americans, e.g. by increasing expenditure on education and requiring equal access to public facilities such as transportation.

● The opportunity to participate in the political process increased black confidence, political awareness and organisational skills.

Negatives

● The proportion of black officials was way below the proportion of Southerners who were black.

● Despite the large number of elected black Republicans, white Republicans dominated state politics in the South.

● No black state governor was elected.

● No Southern state Senate had a black majority and only South Carolina (65 per cent black) had a black majority in the lower house.

● One of the two black US senators, Charles Caldwell of Mississippi, was assassinated by whites.

Some early twentieth-century historians suggested that what they called 'Black Reconstruction' was a period of political domination by illiterate and corrupt black representatives. However, black representatives were neither worse nor better than their white contemporaries. Furthermore, while black representation constituted a political revolution, black Americans never dominated Southern politics because:

● they lacked education, organisation and experience

● they were accustomed to white leadership and domination

● they were in the minority everywhere apart from South Carolina and Mississippi

● the black community was divided (free-born blacks looked down upon ex-slaves)

● the Republican Party was sure of the black vote and favoured white candidates, because they would attract more white votes

● most white Republicans considered black people less competent than whites

● Southern black leaders were usually moderates with no desire to exclude whites from office.

The Civil Rights Act (1875)

In this Act, the Republican-controlled Congress aimed to prevent discrimination in public places such as railroads, hotels and theatres (but not schools). However, the Act was unsuccessful because

● it had been passed by the outgoing Congress, and the new Democrat-influenced Congress was not interested in monitoring legislation that helped the Southern black population

● the burden of enforcement was placed upon black litigants, and litigation was too expensive for most of them

● in 1883, the **Supreme Court** ruled it unconstitutional on the grounds that civil rights issues were the responsibility of each individual state.

! Simple essay style   a

Below is a sample exam-style question. Use your own knowledge and the information on the opposite page to produce a plan for this question. Choose four general points, and provide three pieces of specific information to support each general point. Once you have planned your essay, write the introduction and conclusion for the essay. The introduction should list the points to be discussed in the essay. The conclusion should summarise the key points and justify which point was the most important.

How accurate is it to say that Congressional Reconstruction gave black Americans political equality in the South?

⬍ Spectrum of importance

Below is a sample exam-style question and a list of general points which could be used to answer that question. Use your own knowledge and the information on the opposite page to reach a judgement about the importance of these general points to the question posed.

Write numbers on the spectrum below the list to indicate their relative importance. Having done this, write a brief justification of your placement, explaining why some of these factors are more important than others. The resulting diagram could form the basis of an essay plan.

How far were black Republicans responsible for white Republican domination of Southern politics during Congressional Reconstruction?

1 Black familiarity with white leadership and domination.

2 Black community divisions.

3 Black education, organisation and experience.

4 Black legislators' competence.

5 Black voters.

6 White voters in the South.

⟵——————————————————————⟶

Least important   Most important

The Backlash, part 1

After the Civil War, many white Southerners

- perceived freed black males as dangerous
- continued to believe in black inferiority
- thought the black population intellectually unfit to vote
- felt victimised by Congressional Reconstruction.

These beliefs led Southern whites to adopt violent methods in order to retain control.

The Ku Klux Klan

In 1866, armed white supremacist groups sprang up in most of the old Confederacy. The most famous was Confederate General Nathan Bedford Forrest's Ku Klux Klan. Forrest estimated that the group had around 500,000 members across the South by 1871.

The Ku Klux Klan targeted black officials, schools and churches because Klansmen recognised that office-holding, education and membership of an organisation empowered freed slaves. In Mississippi, the Klan destroyed 25 black schools and murdered 50 black teachers after a Mississippi state law promoted black education in 1870.

Republican-controlled state governments in the South legislated against the Ku Klux Klan but enforcement proved difficult because

- Southern **Democrats** sympathised with the Ku Klux Klan
- it was difficult to convict Klansmen, because they provided alibis for each other and were frequently jury members.

Southern Republican state governors appealed to the US Congress for assistance. Congress responded with the passage of three Enforcement Acts (the Force Acts) in 1870–71. These acts protected the black American right to

- vote
- hold office
- serve on juries
- have equal protection under the law.

The third of the Acts (the Ku Klux Klan Act) gave President Grant the legal and military power to crush the Klan. This ended most of the Klan violence, but others such as the White League continued to use violence and intimidation.

The White League

The first White League was established in Louisiana after a disputed election led a black militia to hold the town of Colfax for a fortnight. Over 100 black Americans were killed in the 'Colfax Massacre' of 1873. The democratically elected government of Louisiana was a Republican regime elected primarily by black voters and protected by federal forces and black militias. However, a government elected by whites and supported by the White League dominated the countryside. In 1874, the Republicans threw out the voting results from many Democrat areas, which led the White League to assassinate several Republican officials and President Grant reluctantly to send in federal troops to help keep the corrupt Republican government in power in Louisiana.

White Leagues soon sprang up in other Southern states. Their declared aim was to maintain public order but in reality they sought to overthrow Republican governments and exclude blacks from public life.

! Complete the paragraph   a

Below is a sample exam-style question and a paragraph written in answer to this question.

The paragraph contains a point and specific examples, but lacks a concluding analytical link back to the question. Complete the paragraph by adding this link back to the question in the space provided.

How significant was the Ku Klux Klan in the years 1865–77?

> The Ku Klux Klan had many supporters and an estimated 500,000 members across the South by 1871. Republican-controlled state governments in the South found it difficult to enforce legislation against the Klan because Klansmen gave each other alibis and served on juries. In 1870, the Klan got away with the destruction of 25 black schools and the murder of 50 black teachers in Mississippi alone. Overall,
>
> _____
>
> _____
>
> _____

! Support or challenge?   a

Below is a sample exam-style question which asks you to what extent you agree with a specific statement. Below that is a list of general statements which are relevant to the question. Using your own knowledge and the information on the opposite page, decide whether these statements support or challenge the statement in question.

How accurate is it to say that Southern white violence achieved little in the years 1865–77?

STATEMENT	SUPPORT	CHALLENGE
The Enforcement Acts gave Grant the power needed to crush the Ku Klux Klan.		
The Ku Klux Klan had 500,000 members by 1871.		
Only a few Klan leaders were tried under the 1871 Ku Klux Klan Act.		
Black militias fought back in black majority areas.		
Republicans struggled to campaign and vote in the face of white violence.		
Northerners were tired of violence and fraud in Southern elections.		

The Backlash, part 2

The incidence of lynching

During the years 1865–77, thousands of black Americans were unlawfully killed (lynched) by whites in majority white areas in the South (black militias often fought back in majority black areas). As lynchings were usually done at night in rural areas, it is difficult to be sure of the exact statistics but large numbers are indicated by the fact that several thousand Ku Klux Klan members were indicted for lynching after the 1871 Ku Klux Klan Act was passed. So many Klansmen were indicted that the federal court system could not cope and only a few leaders were tried. Most were released by 1875.

The restoration of Democrat control in the South

Democrats regained control of the South state by state and quite speedily. By 1877, every Southern state had come under Democrat control: Tennessee (1869), Virginia and North Carolina (1870), Georgia (1871), Texas (1873) Arkansas and Alabama (1874), Louisiana and Mississippi (1876), and finally, Florida and South Carolina (1877). The Democrat-controlled state governments were determined to decrease black economic, social and political power.

The reasons for the restoration of Democrat control in the South were:

- Southern Republicans were increasingly divided along race lines.
- Ex–Confederate soldiers often made it very difficult for Republicans to campaign and vote in Southern states.
- Republican-controlled state governments had taxed heavily in order to help restore the ruined South. Many whites voted Democrat in the hope of tax cuts.

The end of Reconstruction, 1877

Reconstruction ended in the late 1870s for a number of reasons.

- Northerners were exasperated with and bored by the continuing racial violence and fraud in Southern elections, and Grant and many other Northerners wanted to focus upon matters more relevant to the North than the South's racial problems.
- Grant and many other Northern whites had more in common with Southern whites than Southern blacks. Many Northerners were as racist as white Southerners, cared little about the fate of the freed slaves and wanted reconciliation with Southern whites (Grant's 1872 Amnesty Act returned voting and office-holding rights to 150,000 former Confederates).
- The influence of the Radical Republicans in the North had declined as Radical Republican leaders died or retired.
- From 1873, the United States suffered a severe economic **depression** for which voters blamed the Republicans. In 1874, the Democrats gained control of the House of Representatives and this contributed to the growing loss of interest in helping the Southern black population in Congress.
- The Republican Party in the South was weakened by divisions between blacks and whites and by divisions within the races over the spoils of office, and the Democrats had regained control of most of the South.
- In 1877, Republican President Rutherford B. Hayes withdrew all federal troops from the South. Many think that this was a 'deal': Hayes' election was disputed and he needed to gain Democrat acceptance of his presidency.

ⓘ Simple essay style

Below is a sample exam-style question. Use your own knowledge and the information in the section entitled 'Radical Reconstruction 1867–77' to produce a plan for this question. Choose four general points, and provide three pieces of specific information to support each general point. Once you have planned your essay, write the introduction and conclusion for the essay. The introduction should list the points to be discussed in the essay. The conclusion should summarise the key points and justify which point was the most important.

'The end of Reconstruction was due to President Grant.' How far do you agree with this statement?

ⓘ RAG – Rate the timeline

Below is a sample exam-style question and a timeline. Read the question, study the timeline and using three coloured pens, put a red, amber or green star next to the events to show:

Red: events and policies that have no relevance to the question

Amber: events and policies that have some significance to the question

Green: events and policies that are directly relevant to the question

How far do you agree that Reconstruction had effectively ended before 1877?

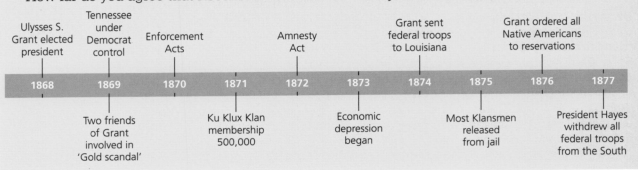

Exam focus

Below is a source, question and sample answer on the events connected with the determination of the US Congress in 1871 to combat the Ku Klux Klan.

Assess the value of the source for revealing white attitudes to black Americans during Reconstruction and the extent of black political power in the South in that period.

Explain your answer, using the source, the information given about its origin and your own knowledge about the historical context.

SOURCE 1

From the testimony given before Congress in 1871 by farmer and stonemason Jack Johnson, a 45-year-old black resident of Laurens County, South Carolina. Johnson gave this testimony before the Joint Select Committee to Enquire into the Condition of Affairs in the Late Insurrectionary States, after he had fled South Carolina. Congress was discussing the need for legislation against the Klan. In 1870, there had been a riot at Laurens County, involving white Democrat voters and black Republican voters.

Q. Were you called on there by the Ku-Klux at any time?

A. Yes sir; I was called on by one man [Mr Reizer] on the way from the riot at Laurens … He says to me, 'What ticket did you vote?' I told him I voted the Republican ticket. 'God Damn you,' says he, ' … you go against our party; you go against us who have been a friend to you all your days. I suppose you hallooed the other day, Hurrah for Governor Scott. Didn't you vote for Governor Scott?' I told him I did, and I thought I was right in doing so … He says, 'Suppose you want to be burned right here?'… he struck me on the head and knocked me down on the face … he beat me to his satisfaction … and he says, 'God Damn you, I've a great mind to shoot you through and through … God Damn you, I left eight of your Republican Party biting up dirt at Laurens, and you will be biting dirt before morning.' … He went on then toward the house to have his horse fed, I struggled … to my wife's house, and she said they had been there hunting me. I told her … I would try to get away from there …

Q. How is it there in regard to the other colored people? Do they feel at liberty to vote as they please, or has this system of intimidation been carried on to any extent?

A. Well, they are down up there now, for all the Republican men that have been the leaders, speaking and going about there, has left there – has come out and left them. My wife come from there about four weeks ago …

Q. Did you do anything else than vote?

A. No sir, only to vote; only this, I took a great propriety in counseling the people which way to vote – the colored people. I had been riding about a great deal. I was the only colored man that had a mule anywhere nigh house, and I would go way off to speeches, and come back and tell the news how the speeches were; that was all I did, and for that they were very down on me.

This source is useful in demonstrating both some differing white attitudes towards black Americans and the extent of black political power. Obviously, it does not give comprehensive coverage of those issues.

Members of the US Congress were sympathetic to Southern black American voters in 1871, as demonstrated by this Joint Select Committee's desire to 'Enquire into the Condition of Affairs in the Late Insurrectionary States'. At this time, Congress was dominated by Northern Republicans and the Republican Party was keen to ensure that it received the black vote in the South. Jack Johnson and the Klansmen Mr Reizer remind us how black votes always went to the Republican Party, so that white Republicans were naturally keen to safeguard the black 'liberty to vote as they please'. Obviously, white Southern Republicans would be grateful for black votes also. So, the source is a valuable and accurate reminder that many Republicans in the North (and by implication in the South), had a sympathetic attitude toward black Americans during Reconstruction – at least as far as their voting was concerned. However, while the source is a valuable reminder that some white Americans had a sympathetic attitude to black Americans in relation to voting, the source is obviously not going to reveal the racist attitude of many whites in both the North and South. At the time that the 15th Amendment was passed, only eight of the Northern states allowed black voting. It is quite likely that even members of the congressional committee had racist attitudes but any racism would have been secondary to their obvious anger at the white people of the 'Late Insurrectionary States' – the committee's official title was a stark reminder of who won and who lost in the Civil War, with the clear implication that Northerners believed these former insurrectionists needed to be carefully watched and controlled.

The source is valuable in revealing the hostile Klan attitude toward the freed slaves. Mr Reizer is furious that a black man dares to vote 'against our party', the Democrat Party, especially as he insists that white people have 'been a friend' to black people 'all your days'. Mr Reizer clearly thinks that the pre-war relationship of master to slave was a paternalistic one – he obviously has a patronising attitude about enslavement. This talk of 'friendship' suggests that Mr Reizer considered slaves incapable of looking after themselves. The source is a valuable reminder that many Southern whites had dramatically changed attitudes to black Americans after the Civil War – Mr Reizer left eight (presumably black) Republicans 'biting dirt' at Laurens, and the indictment of several thousand Klansmen after the Ku Klux Klan Act was passed in 1871 indicates that thousands of black Americans had been lynched since the Civil War. Mr Reizer's feelings about 'our party' are a valuable reflection of the racist attitudes of the Democratic Party, in both the North and the South – the Democrats had the slogan 'This is a white man's government' during the 1868 election. Clearly, the source has considerable value as an accurate reflection of white Democrat attitudes to black Americans. It gives particularly helpful insight into the bitterness that defeated Confederates felt against the race that they perceived as having turned upon them and also against that race's Northern allies – Mr Reizer exhibits understandable hatred of the Northern Republican Governor Robert Kingston Scott, a Pennsylvania-born officer in the Union army. Governor Scott, like his black voter supporters, clearly symbolises the fall of the old Confederate elite.

This is a brief but effective introduction, focused on the question and indicating what the answer will argue.

This paragraph examines the usefulness of the source in reminding us of the positive white Republican attitude to Southern black American voters. The paragraph uses the source and its origin, along with own knowledge, as directed by the question. The writer uses the useful 'descriptive word [sympathetic] + attitude' technique to maintain the focus of the answer and to make a clearly analytical point. The paragraph is balanced in that it gives ways in which the source is both valuable and not valuable – following the 'assess the value' command in the question.

This paragraph examines the hostile attitude of the Ku Klux Klan and members of the Democratic Party. There are appropriate quotations, which are never distracting in length. Source usage and own knowledge are seamlessly combined. The last two sentences summarise the argument of the source, ostentatiously referring back to the keywords in the question – attitude and value.

Mr Reizer and the Democrats were obviously deeply concerned that black Americans had too much political power, whether through the mere act of voting or through their successful contribution to the election of Republicans such as Governor Scott. In a way, the fact that the US Congress is concerned to monitor the 'system of intimidation' also suggests considerable black political power – Southern black voters have two branches of the federal government on their side in 1871, the legislature (Congress) and the executive (President Ulysses S. Grant). Johnson's testimony is a useful reminder of the empowering nature of the franchise – there is more than rudimentary black political organisation here, in that Johnson has ridden around 'counseling the people in which way to vote', and telling everyone the message contained in the speeches he has gone 'way off' to hear. This demonstration of black political organisational capacity certainly frightened the Ku Klux Klan – it was a major reason for their establishment and obviously why 'they were very down on me'. When Johnson talks about 'all the Republican men that have been leaders' and forced to flee as he was, one wonders whether they were members of the Union League, an important element in the Republican Party in the South. This source is a valuable reminder that black Americans sometimes had considerable political clout in the South – Mr Reizer certainly thought so. There is statistical proof of a considerable degree of black political power in the South in the years following the Civil War. The 700,000 black voters in the South outnumbered the 600,000 white voters – at least, prior to Grant's Amnesty Act of 1872, which restored the franchise to over 100,000 former Confederate officials. Between 1869 and 1877, there were 16 black congressmen and two black senators elected to the US Congress, and over 700 men served in the state legislatures. Of course, whites dominated the Republican Party, so that this was not 'Black Reconstruction' – but, to a large extent, blacks had political power in the post-war South.

On the other hand, the source is also a useful reminder that in some places – in Laurens County at the very least – there were limits on the extent of black political power. Prior to the Force Acts, violent white supremacists such as the Ku Klux Klan were often effective in stopping black voting – so much so that Jack Johnson had to flee South Carolina. It seems that Johnson lived and travelled in rural areas, and that is where black communities were most vulnerable to lynching. However, South Carolina was a majority black state, and in majority black areas, black militias frequently had success in fending off white supremacist attacks. It may be that the congressional committee was out to make the case for the Force Acts, and in some ways it might be argued that they were overemphasising the power of the Klan and perhaps giving a false impression of the extent of black political power.

Overall, the source is a useful reminder of Northern white Republican and Southern white Democrat attitudes toward black Americans, but perhaps less useful on the extent of black power, because it focuses on the limitations on the exercise of that power.

The first sentence of this paragraph follows on from the last paragraph and connects the two enquiries in the question. As in the two preceding paragraphs, there is a summarising sentence referring back to the question. There is a pointed reference to the 'Black Reconstruction' debate in the question.

This paragraph gives the other side of the argument presented in the previous paragraph, but it is probably the weakest paragraph, as the second half of the paragraph goes back to the argument that black Americans did have considerable power.

This is a brief but adequate conclusion to the argument the answer has followed about the two enquiries.

This is a good answer. The candidate engages with the question and analyses the source material quite effectively. There is clear evidence of evaluation and it is evident that the candidate is weighing the evidence and attempting to discuss in a reasoned way what can be said on the basis of it. The candidate is clearly aware of the wider context and attempts to integrate this into the answer. The candidate attempts to offer a valid (if limited) conclusion.

Range of explanation

It would be useful to look at this answer through the eyes of the examiner. The examiner will look for a range of explanation. In the margin, write words or phrases that sum up the contents of the arguments of that paragraph. Good answers present at least three explanations and discuss each one in a separate paragraph.

2 The triumph of 'Jim Crow', 1883–c1990

The impact of the Civil Rights Cases (1883) in the Supreme Court

Background

During Reconstruction, black American rights had been advanced thanks to the 13th, 14th and 15th Amendments:

- the 13th Amendment ended slavery
- the 14th Amendment declared black American citizenship
- the 15th Amendment enfranchised black males.

These black rights had been sustained by the Republican-dominated Congress, by President Ulysses S. Grant, and by the federal government's armed forces in the South.

However, the majority of Southern whites resented such black advancement from the first and had sought ways to deprive black Americans of their newly granted civil rights. Southern whites used several methods to combat black advances:

- While the federal government remained sympathetic to black Americans in the South, frustrated white Southerners focused upon violence, e.g. the Ku Klux Klan and the White League.
- When it became clear that the federal government and the Republican Party were losing interest in the South, white Southerners began to change their focus to segregation.

This new focus on segregation led to several Supreme Court rulings that supported Southern white discriminatory practice.

The Supreme Court was sympathetic to states' rights and the right of Southern states to determine their race relations was slowly restored in a series of Supreme Court rulings in the last quarter of the nineteenth century. The first such ruling was in the Slaughter-House Cases of 1873, in which the Supreme Court ruled that the 14th Amendment was not designed to transfer control over civil rights issues from the states to the federal government.

The Slaughter-House Cases had not directly involved black Americans but the ruling on states' rights impacted upon them in that it encouraged Southern white racists to use the authority of their states to deprive black Americans of their civil rights. The next significant Supreme Court ruling that directly involved black Americans was the ruling on the Civil Rights Cases of 1883.

What the Supreme Court ruled in the Civil Rights Cases (1883)

In 1883, the Supreme Court reviewed five similar civil rights cases in which black Americans had sued transportation companies, hotels and theatres because of exclusion from 'white only' areas. The Supreme Court declared the Civil Rights Act (1875) and federal government intervention over racial discrimination on the part of private individuals and organisations to be unconstitutional.

The impact of the Civil Rights Cases ruling

The Supreme Court's ruling in the Civil Rights Cases had a negative impact on the black situation:

- Justice John Marshall Harlan, the sole dissenter in the case, said the ruling endorsed segregation and constituted 'a badge of servitude' that contravened the 13th Amendment.
- Most white Americans, including Congress, were unmoved by this loss of black civil rights.
- The Southern states were empowered to erode the rights black Americans had gained during Reconstruction. During the 1880s, *de jure* segregation in the form of the **Jim Crow laws** was introduced in all areas of Southern life.

Write the question **a**

Having read the opposite page,
The following source is an extract from Justice John Marshall Harlan's dissent to the 1883 Supreme Court ruling on the Civil Rights Cases. Having read the opposite page, write an exam-style question using the source. Remember, the question must focus on two enquiries.

Assess the value of the source for revealing

_____

and

_____

Explain your answer, using the source, the information given about its origin, and your own knowledge about the historical context.

SOURCE 1

From Justice John Marshall Harlan's dissent to the 1883 Supreme Court ruling on the Civil Rights Cases. Kentucky-born Harlan supported the Union in the Civil War but also supported slavery and opposed the Emancipation Proclamation. However, he became a strong supporter of civil rights after the Civil War. He was known as 'The Great Dissenter' because he dissented from the majority opinion in the Civil Rights Cases and also in Plessy v. Ferguson (1896).

... I cannot resist the conclusion that the substance and spirit of the recent amendments of the Constitution have been sacrificed by a subtle and ingenious verbal criticism ...

The purpose of the first section of the act of Congress of ... 1875, was to prevent race discrimination in respect of the accommodations and facilities of inns, public conveyances, and places of public amusement. It ... declares that ... conditions and limitations, whatever they may be, shall not be applied so as to work a discrimination solely because of race, color, or previous condition of servitude. The second section provides a penalty against anyone denying, or aiding or inciting the denial, of any citizen, of that equality of right given by the first section except for reasons by law applicable to citizens of every race or color and regardless of any previous condition of servitude.

Congress has not, in these matters, entered the domain of State control and supervision. It does not, as I have said, assume to prescribe the general conditions and limitations under which inns, public conveyances, and places of public amusement shall be conducted or managed. It simply declares, in effect, that, since the nation has established universal freedom in this country for all time, there shall be no discrimination, based merely upon race or color, in respect of the accommodations and advantages of public conveyances, inns, and places of public amusement ...

There seems to be no substantial difference between my brethren and myself as to the purpose of Congress ... The effect of the statute, the court says, is that colored citizens, whether formerly slaves or not, and citizens of other races shall have the same accommodations and privileges in all inns, public conveyances, and places of amusement as are enjoyed by white persons, and vice versa ...

I am of the opinion that such discrimination practised by corporations and individuals in the exercise of their public or quasi-public functions is a badge of servitude the imposition of which Congress may prevent under its power, by appropriate legislation, to enforce the Thirteenth Amendment; and consequently, without reference to its enlarged power under the Fourteenth Amendment, the act of March 1, 1875, is not, in my judgment, repugnant to the Constitution...

The spread of Jim Crow laws

As soon as the Civil War ended, white Southerners introduced segregation. The desire for the physical separation of blacks and whites in public places was common to most white Americans. Even the Republican-controlled Congress was sympathetic: at the same time that it passed the 14th Amendment it also authorised segregated schooling in Washington DC.

De facto segregation (segregation in fact if not in law) slowly developed into *de jure* segregation (segregation in law) as Southern whites grew increasingly fearful and resentful of growing black self-confidence and success (for example, the proportion of black farm owners had risen from 3.8% in 1880 to 25% by 1900) and increasingly assured of federal government acquiescence.

Southern whites were able to introduce segregation laws because the American Constitution had given the states power over

- voting
- education
- law enforcement
- transportation.

The segregation laws passed by the Southern states became known as the Jim Crow laws (Jim Crow was a popular black comic figure in nineteenth-century entertainment). The Jim Crow laws were sustained because the federal government had lost interest in the black American predicament and the Supreme Court was particularly sympathetic to Southern whites and states' rights.

The Jim Crow 'color line' was first set down in law in public transport because large-scale railroad expansion in the South in the 1870s forced railroad companies and customers to consider the issue of blacks and whites sitting close together.

Changes to rail travel in Florida, 1887

The Black Codes often ordered segregated railroad cars, but railroad cars were increasingly integrated during Congressional Reconstruction. The end of Reconstruction saw the spread of *de jure* segregation on railroad cars, as demonstrated in a Florida state law of 1887. The Florida state legislators were obviously encouraged and emboldened by the Supreme Court's ruling in the Civil Rights Cases of 1883, which had declared the Civil Rights Act (1875) to be unconstitutional. Other Southern states passed similar laws.

The extension of segregation to other social areas

During the 1880s, *de jure* segregation was introduced in all areas of Southern life. Southern states and cities passed segregation laws that separated blacks and whites in trains, streetcars, stations, theatres, churches, parks, schools, restaurants and cemeteries. All aspects of society were covered: whites were not supposed to use black prostitutes and the races were not allowed to play checkers together. The Southern states passed segregation laws at varying speeds and with varying consistency and there was no opposition from the federal government in Washington DC.

⚠ Spot the mistake

Below is a sample exam-style question and a paragraph written in answer to this question. Why does this paragraph not get high praise? What is wrong with the focus of the answer in this paragraph?

> How far do you agree that Southern whites restored white supremacy after the Civil War through violence?

Southern whites used several methods to restore white supremacy after the Civil War. In that war, the Northern states had fought the South, where whites had maintained white supremacy through the institution of slavery. Southern whites did indeed use violence against black Americans, but they also took advantage of the powers reserved to states in the American Constitution when they introduced *de jure* segregation. Under the Jim Crow laws, black Americans were segregated in public places such as railroad cars and schools. Southern whites were aided in the imposition of the Jim Crow laws by the federal government's lack of interest in the black American situation down South.

⚡ Develop the detail

Below is a sample exam-style question and a paragraph written in answer to this question. The paragraph contains a limited amount of detail. Annotate the paragraph to add additional detail to the answer.

> To what extent was the spread of the Jim Crow laws due to the nature of the federal system of government?

The spread of the Jim Crow laws owed a great deal to the federal system of government. The American Constitution had reserved great powers to the individual states. However, it was Southern white racism that was the main reason for the introduction of *de jure* segregation. Once the slaves were freed, whites became very conscious of the issue of blacks and whites in close proximity in public places. The expansion of railroad travel in the 1870s brought the issue to prominence and states began to introduce *de jure* segregation on railroad cars. The Jim Crow laws then spread to other areas of Southern life.

Excluding black voters

Southern whites argued that as Congressional Reconstruction was a period of irresponsible and unintelligent black rule, black Americans should be disfranchised. This was done gradually and through a variety of methods during the 1880s and 1890s. States such as Mississippi and Louisiana provide good illustrations of the methods by which black voters were excluded.

Discrimination in Mississippi from 1890, and Louisiana's 'grandfather clause' (1898)

Mississippi and Louisiana excluded black voters through several methods:

1 White supremacist groups used violence against black voters. In Mississippi, the 'Red Shirts' was a paramilitary group that some described as the military arm of the Democratic Party. It intimidated black voters after its establishment in 1875.

2 The re-drawing of congressional districts decreased black representation. For example, the Democratic Party redrew congressional districts in Mississippi after Reconstruction. They created a 'shoestring' district that ran the length of the Mississippi River and took in the black-majority areas of the Mississippi Delta. The aim was to decrease black voting power in other constituencies.

3 Fraud was common. For example, white Mississippi voting officials claimed that mules ate the ballot papers from black majority counties.

4 Mississippi and Louisiana introduced poll taxes. Georgia had been the first Southern state to do so – as early as 1871. As black Americans were amongst the poorest inhabitants of the South, they were disproportionately affected by having to pay tax in order to vote.

5 In 1890, Mississippi became the first Southern state to call a constitutional convention with the aim of excluding black voters. Mississippi introduced literacy and income qualifications. Other Southern states followed – South Carolina (1895), Louisiana (1898), and Alabama and Virginia (1902). Georgia was the last state to do so (1908). White Southern registrars manipulated the literacy tests e.g. they asked would-be black voters to explain a particular section of the state constitution.

6 In 1898, Louisiana sought to help poor white voters who could not afford the poll tax or pass the literacy test. This was achieved through 'grandfather clauses', which said a man could vote if he or an ancestor had voted before Reconstruction. That enabled poor whites to vote but excluded black Americans, very few of whom had been able to vote before Reconstruction. Other states followed Louisiana's example.

7 After Reconstruction, the South was developing into a single-party region. Southern white Democrats introduced the white primary, in which voters chose between Democrat candidates for office. When black Americans were excluded from white primaries, they were deprived of the opportunity to secure the election of black or sympathetic public officials.

The impact on voter numbers in the South in the 1890s

The methods used by states such as Louisiana and Mississippi to exclude black voters had a dramatic impact on black voting numbers. Within two years of Mississippi's adoption of a new constitution, the number of black voters in the state fell from around 190,000 to around 8,000. When the federal government did not challenge Mississippi's actions, other Southern states were emboldened. In 1896, 130,334 black men voted in Louisiana, but after Louisiana introduced a new state constitution in 1898, only 1,400 voted in 1904.

! Delete as applicable a

Below are a sample exam-style question and a paragraph written in answer to this question. Read the paragraph and decide which of the possible options (in bold) is most appropriate. Delete the least appropriate options and complete the paragraph by justifying your selection.

How successful were Southern white attempts to exclude black voters in the years 1883–1900?

White Southerners used several methods to exclude black voters and these were successful to a **great/fair/limited extent**. Within two years of Mississippi's adoption of a new constitution, the number of black voters in the state fell from around 190,000 to around 8,000. When the federal government did not challenge Mississippi's actions, other Southern states were emboldened. In 1896, 130,334 black men voted in Louisiana, but after Louisiana introduced a new state constitution in 1898, only 1,400 voted in 1904. Clearly, Southern attempts to exclude black voters were **extremely/moderately/slightly successful** because

_____

_____

! Mind map

Use the information on the page opposite to add detail to the mind map below to show the causes of the exclusion of black voters.

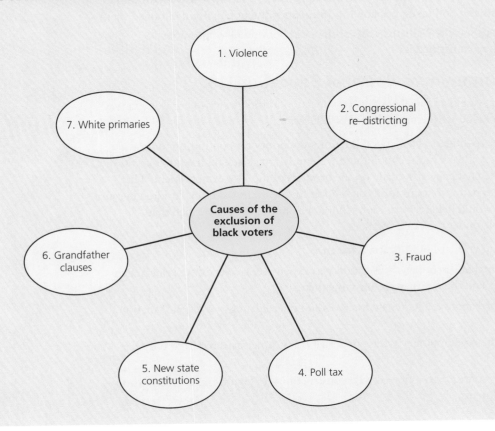

1. Violence

2. Congressional re–districting

7. White primaries

Causes of the exclusion of black voters

6. Grandfather clauses

3. Fraud

5. New state constitutions

4. Poll tax

Three significant Supreme Court rulings

The impact of Plessy v. Ferguson (1896)

After the Civil Rights Cases, the Supreme Court issued several other rulings that suggested federal support for the segregation imposed by the white Southern state governments.

In Plessy v. Ferguson, the Supreme Court ruled that 'separate but equal' facilities for blacks and whites on public transportation were not against the 14th Amendment. The court declared legislation 'powerless to eradicate racial instincts'.

Plessy v. Ferguson had a negative impact on black Americans, as noted by the sole dissenter, Justice Harlan. Harlan criticised his colleagues for relegating black Americans to a 'condition of legal inferiority'. While some black Americans would have been satisfied with separate but equal, the facilities were never equal and the Supreme Court did nothing to ensure that they were. For example, Southern states spent 10 times more on white schools than on black schools.

The impact of Williams v. Mississippi (1898)

In Williams v. Mississippi, the black defendant challenged his indictment for murder on the grounds that the state of Mississippi unconstitutionally excluded black Americans from grand juries (jurors had to be qualified voters and Mississippi's 1890 constitution excluded black voters). Williams claimed that the voting qualifications had been adopted for purposes of discrimination and gave registrars excessive power. The Supreme Court ruled that the literacy test and poll tax provisions in the Mississippi state constitution were not discriminatory, on the grounds that they were not mentioned in the 15th Amendment.

The Williams v. Mississippi ruling had a negative impact upon the Southern black population because:

- The Supreme Court was not upholding the 15th Amendment.
- The ruling reflected the contemporary white belief in black American unfitness to vote.
- The ruling demonstrated skilful Southern white manipulation of the law – it was cunning to introduce literacy tests and poll taxes, because the 15th Amendment had not mentioned them.
- Supreme Court rulings such as Williams v. Mississippi did not initiate or promote discrimination but they confirmed it.

The impact of Cumming v. Board of Education (1899)

The sole Supreme Court case over racial equality in education in the Plessy v. Ferguson era was Cumming v. Richmond County [Georgia] Board of Education.

Cumming and his black co-litigants challenged Richmond County for continuing to fund a white high school but not a black high school (there were only four black high schools across the whole of the South). The challenge was made on the grounds of the 14th Amendment. The county argued that it was better to focus funds on schools for the youngest black children because only a few went to and would benefit from high school. The Supreme Court ruled that inequality was reasonable under the circumstances.

The impact of Cumming v. Board of Education was that:

- black litigants were further discouraged (litigation was expensive, lawyers were reluctant to represent black clients and the courts were unsympathetic)
- the Supreme Court had approved segregated schools and once again given federal sanction to the Jim Crow laws
- the ruling reflected the contemporary white view that black Americans required only a limited education
- the South was able to continue to ignore the Reconstruction-era civil rights legislation and constitutional amendments.

Identify the concept a

Below are sample exam-style questions based on some of the following concepts:

Cause questions concern the reasons for something, or why something happened.

Consequence questions concern the impact of an event, and action or a policy.

Change/continuity questions ask you to investigate the extent to which things changed or stayed the same.

Similarities/difference questions ask you to investigate the extent to which two events, actions or policies were similar.

Significance questions concern the importance of an event, and action or a policy.

Read each of the questions and work out which of the concepts they are based upon.

'Black American civil rights were fundamentally weakened by Plessy v. Ferguson.' How far do you agree with this statement?

How far did the status of black Americans change between 1865 and 1900?

How accurate is it to say that the most important result of Plessy v. Ferguson was the segregation of public transportation?

How far did Supreme Court rulings contribute to the establishment of Jim Crow laws?

To what extent was black American status in 1900 superior to black American status under slavery?

You're the examiner a

Below is a sample exam-style question and a paragraph written in answer to this question. Read the paragraph and the mark scheme provided on pages 106–7. Decide which level you would award the paragraph. Write the level below, along with a justification for your choice.

How accurate is it to say that Plessy v. Ferguson relegated black Americans to a condition of legal inferiority?

> Justice Harlan accused his colleagues of relegating black Americans to a condition of legal inferiority in Plessy v. Ferguson. Had 'separate but equal' been adhered to, black Americans would not have suffered legal inferiority. Black Americans had often made it clear that they were comfortable with separate but equal accommodation. For example, after Florida passed a law mandating segregation on Florida's railroads, black ministers in Jacksonville told their congregations to boycott lines that did not provide equal facilities for black passengers. That suggests that separate was not a problem, but equal was. However, Justice Harlan surely knew the fate of the 'equal' provisions in such state legislation, and was therefore correct to say that Plessy v. Ferguson made the Supreme Court appear complicit in segregated AND unequal facilities.

Level:

_____

Mark:

_____

Reason for choosing this level and this mark:

_____

_____

Exam focus

Below is a sample answer on the situation of black Americans between 1865 and 1900. Read the answer to the exam-style question and the comments around it.

How far do you agree that the deterioration in the status of Southern black Americans in the late nineteenth century was primarily due to Northern Republicans?

During the 1880s and 1890s, the Southern states introduced segregation and disfranchisement with varying speed and consistency. The deterioration in the status of black Americans was due to the changing position of the Northern Republicans, to the actions of the federal government, to the Democratic Party, to the American Constitution's states' rights provisions and to contemporary white opinion. However, the single most important factor was the Southern white determination to maintain white supremacy and Northern white sympathy for that determination.

This introduction establishes the factors causing the deterioration and makes it clear which one the essay will argue to be the most important.

Northern Republicans contributed to improvements then to deterioration in the status of Southern blacks. They were the major force behind the passage of the 13th, 14th and 15th Amendments. However, by the late 1870s they had tired of violent and fraudulent Southern elections and they shared Southern white Republican impatience with black party members. Furthermore, Westward expansion decreased the importance of the Southern black vote. Democrats and particularly Southern Democrats bore equal blame for the deterioration in the status of Southern black Americans. Democrats had declared themselves to be the white man's party in the 1868 election and they never moved from that position. Overall, both parties bore equal responsibility for the deterioration of the black Americans' situation. Both ensured that Congress failed to uphold its own 1875 Civil Rights Act.

This paragraph explores the specified factor, Northern Republicans, and attributes blame to Republicans and Democrats.

Three Northern Republican presidents ignored the black predicament after Reconstruction. Grant strongly supported the 15th Amendment, but also sought reconciliation with Southern whites. In 1872, he promoted the Amnesty Act, which restored the vote to over 1,000 former high-ranking Confederate officials. In 1877, Hayes' withdrawal of federal troops from the South signalled Republican willingness to allow the restoration of Southern white and Democrat supremacy. In 1881, Garfield admitted that he 'never could get in love with [the black] creatures'. Successive Republican presidents therefore bore some responsibility for the deterioration in black Americans status, although not as much as the political parties: a president alone could do little in the face of congressional opposition.

This paragraph tries to assess the extent of presidential responsibility, taking care to compare two factors – president and parties/Congress.

The judicial branch of the federal government played an important part in the spread of the Jim Crow laws and black disfranchisement. A series of Supreme Court rulings undermined the 14th and 15th Amendments. In the Civil Rights Cases (1883), the Supreme Court ruled the 1875 Civil Rights Act unconstitutional. In Plessy v. Ferguson (1896), the court ruled 'separate but equal' constitutional, but separate facilities in the South were never equal. In Williams v. Mississippi (1898), the court effectively approved black disfranchisement, and in Cumming v. Board of Education (1899), it sanctioned inequality in education expenditure as reasonable because few black children attended high school (they had little opportunity to do so). While the Supreme Court did not initiate the decline in black status, it certainly supported it.

This paragraph explores the Supreme Court as a factor, and leads back to the arguments of the introduction.

Contemporary white opinion underlay the other reasons for the deterioration in black status. When Republicans, Democrats, Congress, presidents and the Supreme Court abandoned Southern blacks, it was because they shared the contemporary white belief in black inferiority. Southern whites were determined and ingenious in implementing their white supremacist views. As Northerners increasingly lost interest in the South, Southern whites decreased their use of violence and used an ingenious variety of methods to ensure a deterioration in black political status. In Mississippi, Democrats re-drew congressional districts to decrease black voting power, officials claimed mules had eaten black votes, and the 1890 constitution introduced income and literacy qualifications to legalise black disfranchisement. Georgia had introduced the poll tax as early as 1871. Such ruses had no mention in the 15th Amendment so it was feasible to argue that it did not prohibit them. Louisiana ensured these ruses did not penalise poor whites through the grandfather clause (1898), which allowed a man to vote if he or an ancestor had voted before the Civil War. That excluded most black Americans. By 1900, the South had become a single-party state and the introduction of white primaries ensured that black voters had no say in the selection of Democrat candidates for office.

> This paragraph focuses on the importance of white opinion as a cause of black disfranchisement.

White opinion was also behind the spread of *de jure* segregation that signalled the deterioration in black social status. Southern whites had never wanted to share public space with black Americans, as shown in the Black Codes passed in 1865–66. There was some integration during Reconstruction, as on the railroads, but the end of Reconstruction saw the spread of the Jim Crow laws, as in Florida's 1887 law mandating segregated railroad cars.

> This paragraph focuses on white opinion as a cause of the spread of the Jim Crow laws.

Segregation and black disfranchisement owed much to the rights reserved to states in the American Constitution of 1787. Late-nineteenth century white Americans were generally sympathetic toward the states' rights enshrined in their beloved Constitution. This was demonstrated in the Supreme Court's ruling that the 1875 Civil Rights Act was unconstitutional because the federal government had no right to intervene when individuals and organisations were discriminatory, and in the lack of congressional opposition to that ruling.

> This paragraph explores the role of belief in states' rights in the deterioration.

Overall though, white racism was the most important factor in the deterioration of black Americans' status. It underlay the loss of interest in the fate of black Southerners on the part of Northern Republicans and the three branches of the federal government. Even if Northern Republicans and all other Northerners had not lost interest in the South's race problems, diehard Southern white racists would have continued to use violence, the Democratic Party would have continued to collude with them and black Americans would have found it difficult to sustain their civil rights.

> This conclusion reaffirms the essay's argument that the main factor behind the deterioration was widely shared white racism and 'removes' factors to try to justify the essay's argument on the main factor.

This is a good essay. The range of factors identified and supported in this answer demonstrates a high level of appropriate knowledge. The importance of the specified factor (Northern Republicans) is weighed up against the importance of the other factors throughout the essay. There is an attempt to reach a judgement.

Maintaining focus

This essay is successful because it manages a strong focus on the question throughout. Every single paragraph is focused on possible explanations for the deterioration in the status of Southern black Americans. Go through the essay and underline every mention of the words 'deterioration' and 'status'. Next, look at an essay you have written and underline your use of keywords. Can you improve on your own efforts in the light of what you have seen here?

3 The New Deal and race relations, 1933–41

The influence of Southern whites in the Democratic Party REVISED

In the years between the end of Reconstruction (c1877) and 1932, the three branches of the federal government did little or nothing to aid black Americans. The situation did not look particularly promising for black Americans in 1933:

- The Supreme Court was dominated by conservative justices.
- The United States had a new president, the Democrat **Franklin Roosevelt**, whose main concern was to obtain congressional cooperation in getting the country out of the economic depression.
- White voters across the nation were anxious about the Depression and not particularly interested in the plight of black Americans.
- White Southern Democrat conservatives had great influence in the US Congress.

In 1933, the Democratic Party was a loose coalition containing:

- urban (mostly Catholic) ethnic voters in the North
- workers and middle-class liberals across America
- the 'Solid South', where all whites voted Democrat.

The South's single-party system led to the repeated re-election of the same Democrat candidates, who were invariably more conservative than Democrats in the rest of America. This enabled long-serving conservative Southern Democrat senators and representatives to gain disproportionate influence in the US Congress under seniority rules that gave them over half the committee chairmanships and control of key committees.

Southern white Democrat influence on congressional committees enabled them to block legislation that would help black Americans. The result was that Congress failed to address black grievances in the years 1933–41.

The failure to address black grievances

Black Americans across the nation had many grievances in 1933.

Northern black Americans suffered from political, social, economic and legal disadvantages:

- They could vote, but they never won state-wide office because many whites would only vote for white candidates.
- *De facto* segregation kept black Americans confined to crowded ghettos, e.g. New York City's Harlem, Chicago's South Side.
- Despite a slowly growing black middle class, most black Americans were poor and disproportionately affected by the Depression.
- There were occasional lynchings, and **Malcom X**'s brother said there was little difference between the way police in the South and police in Michigan treated black Americans.

Black Americans in the South had even more grievances over their political, social, economic and legal disadvantages:

- Most were employed in relatively unskilled work such as sharecropping and domestic service, and poor education in underfunded segregated schools made economic advancement difficult.
- They suffered *de jure* segregation in public places. The Jim Crow laws remained firmly entrenched and enforced.
- Most were excluded from voting because of difficult literacy tests, the expense of the poll tax and the threat of violence and/or intimidation. Black Southerners lacked representation because the segregationist white Democratic Party dominated Southern politics and offices.
- Whites dominated law enforcement and black Americans lacked protection under the law. Lynching remained an issue: over 1,200 black Americans were lynched in the South in the years 1901–29.

! Mind map

Use the information on the opposite page to create your own mind map to show the ways in which both black Northerners and black Southerners lacked equality in the United States in 1933.

◉ Identify an argument   **a**

Below are a series of definitions, a sample exam-style question and two sample paragraphs. One of the paragraphs achieves a high mark because it contains an argument. The other achieves a lower mark because it contains only description and assertion. Identify which is which. The mark scheme on pages 104–5 will help you.

Description: a detailed account.

Assertion: a statement of fact or an opinion which is not supported by reason.

Reason: a statement which explains or justifies something.

Argument: an assertion justified with a reason.

How far do you agree that black grievances in 1933 were primarily a Southern issue?

Black grievances were clearly primarily a Southern issue. While the Northern black population had the vote, most of the Southern black population was excluded from voting because of difficult literacy tests, the expense of the poll tax and the threat of violence and/or intimidation. Black Southerners lacked representation because the segregationist white Democratic Party dominated Southern politics and offices.

Although Southern black Americans were more disadvantaged than black Americans in the North, the black population across the nation was in an inferior political position. While most black Southerners were excluded from voting by means of literacy tests, the poll tax and violence and intimidation, Northern black candidates never won state-wide office because many whites would only vote for white candidates. The Southern situation was clearly worse: black Southerners had no say in local or national government. However, Northern black political inferiority was clearly an issue, because even with the vote and the ability to vote for sympathetic white officials, black Northerners had a justifiable grievance in that in a representative chamber containing 100 elected officials in a country in which black Americans constituted over 10 per cent of the population, there was not a single black Senator. This demonstrated nationwide white racism. Clearly, black political inequality was a nationwide issue, not merely a Southern one, although the situation was obviously far worse in the South.

The failure to address black grievances

Continuation of the Jim Crow laws

President Roosevelt said little about the Jim Crow laws because he did not want to alienate Southern white Democrats, but his activist wife **Eleanor Roosevelt** ostentatiously signalled her support for black Americans in the South.

The Jim Crow laws were a constant reminder of black inferiority. Young **Martin Luther King Jr** was the son of a respected black minister in Atlanta, Georgia. If he wanted to travel on the bus, it had to be in the section reserved for black Americans at the back of the bus. He could not buy a soda or a hotdog from the downtown store lunch counter. He had to drink from the 'colored' water fountain, use the 'colored' restroom, and sit in the inferior 'colored' section of any movie theatres. When Eleanor Roosevelt attended a biracial meeting in the South in 1938, Birmingham's police chief, **Bull Connor**, tried to stop her sitting next to black delegates.

Exclusion of black voters

In 1941, only 3 per cent of eligible black voters were registered to vote in the South. Would-be black voters were deterred by

- violence
- intimidation
- literacy tests
- the poll tax.

In 1937, Nolan Breedlove, a 28-year-old white man, tried to get the Supreme Court to outlaw the poll tax, but the court upheld Georgia's annual one dollar poll tax. In 1943, **Rosa Parks**, a politically aware black woman, 'failed' the literacy test in Montgomery, Alabama. She was finally allowed to register in 1945, but had to pay an expensive $16.50 poll tax.

The inability to vote gave Southern blacks no chance to elect sympathetic officials. Without sympathetic legislators, neither state legislatures nor the US Congress were able to pass legislation to improve black American status. The **National Association for the Advancement of Colored People (NAACP)** demanded an end to the poll tax, but although President Franklin Roosevelt criticised it, he did not work to end it.

The defeat of federal attempts at anti-lynching legislation

Anti-lynching bills were repeatedly defeated in Congress thanks to the influence of Southern Democrats.

The NAACP campaigned for anti-lynching legislation and in the 1920s it had found a congressional ally in Republican Representative Leonidas Dyer, whose St Louis district contained increasing numbers of black Americans. Southern Democrats used a variety of tactics to ensure the defeat of his bills in 1919, 1922, 1923 and 1924, but the publicity might have contributed to a decline in lynching.

In 1934, the NAACP supported Senators Costigan of Colorado and Wagner of New York when they introduced an anti-lynching bill. Their bill was killed by a Southern Democrat **filibuster**. Later that year, the lynching of black American Claude Neal in Florida was nationwide headline news. Neal was tortured for two hours in front of an enthusiastic white crowd. This prompted a second Costigan–Wagner bill. The Roosevelt administration, anxious not to alienate Southern Democrats, did not support the bill, which was killed off by a seven-week Southern Democrat filibuster. That filibuster was stopping other important **New Deal** legislation from being considered and passed, so the Roosevelt administration did nothing to try to save the bill. Another anti-lynching bill met a similar fate in 1937.

Simple essay style

Below is a sample exam-style question. Use your own knowledge and the information on the opposite page to produce a plan for this question. Choose four general points, and provide three pieces of specific information to support each general point. Once you have planned your essay, write the introduction and conclusion for the essay. The introduction should list the points to be discussed in the essay. The conclusion should summarise the key points and justify which point was the most important.

'The failure to address black grievances in the years 1933–41 was due to the economic depression.' How far do you agree with this statement?

Turning assertion into argument

Below is a sample exam-style question and a series of assertions. Read the exam question and then add a justification to each of the assertions to turn it into an argument.

How significant were the Costigan-Wagner anti-lynching bills?

The Costigan-Wagner bills posed a significant challenge to Southern white supremacy because . . .

The Costigan-Wagner bills did not pose a significant challenge to Southern white supremacy because . . .

The Claude Neal lynching was particularly important because . . .

It can be seen that Southern white Democrats had disproportionate influence in Congress because . . .

Impact of the New Deal, part 1

Background

The New York stock market collapse of 1929 triggered several years of economic depression. Black Americans were already poorer than white Americans and less likely to have marketable skills so the Great Depression hit them far harder than it hit white Americans:

- When crop prices plummeted, thousands of Southern black farmers left the land and migrated to the cities, but urban black unemployment averaged 45 per cent. Desperate whites moved into the unskilled jobs traditionally held by black Americans – domestic service, street cleaning, garbage collection and bell hops. White vigilante groups such as Atlanta's Black Shirts often prevented black employment. The black unemployment rate was generally five times higher than that of whites.
- Unskilled black workers were generally last hired and first fired.
- There was no effective social security system so some black Americans were starving.

Whites also suffered. In 1932, 25 per cent of the American workforce was unemployed. So, when Franklin Roosevelt became president in March 1933, he proposed a New Deal to help alleviate the impact of the Depression. He sought and obtained unprecedented powers and funding from Congress and used it to establish agencies to help the poor and unemployed. There were many agencies, each with different initials. These 'alphabet agencies' had a varying impact on black Americans.

Effects of the AAA on black farmers

The federal government considered overproduction to be the greatest problem of American agriculture so the Agricultural Adjustment Act (AAA) of May 1933 invited farmers to voluntarily decrease their production in exchange for government subsidies.

The AAA had a disadvantageous effect on Southern black farmers:

- At local level, the implementation of the AAA was dominated by the most powerful landowners who controlled the county committees, and they usually supported discriminatory treatment of black farmers.
- When large landowners had the opportunity to make money by removing land from production, they evicted sharecroppers and tenants. In 1933, 87 per cent of the 800,000 black American farmers were tenants or sharecroppers. Between 1933 and 1940, roughly 200,000 black sharecroppers were evicted.
- Until 1936, federal compensation due to evicted tenants and sharecroppers was distributed by white landowners who frequently kept it for themselves. After 1936, the federal government made out cheques to individual black workers, but many white landowners intimidated black workers into signing over the cheques.
- Many large landowners used AAA subsidies to buy machinery that replaced black workers.
- When additional labour was needed for planting and harvesting, large landowners persuaded local relief officials to remove black Americans from the welfare rolls so that desperation would force them to accept very low wages.

President Roosevelt wanted Southern Democrat support for his New Deal, so he did little to ensure that the AAA was helpful rather than harmful to black Americans in the South. A 1936 NAACP report complained that six million black agricultural workers received no federal aid – although that situation subsequently improved.

(i) Establish criteria a

Below is a sample exam-style question which requires you to make a judgement. The key term in the question has been underlined. Defining the meaning of the key term can help you establish criteria that you can use to make a judgement.

Read the question, define the key term and then set out two or three criteria based on the key term, which you can use to reach and justify a judgement.

How accurate is it to say that powerful landowners were the main <u>reason for the suffering of Southern black farmers</u> during the Depression?

Definition

_____

_____

Criteria to judge the extent to which powerful landowners were primarily responsible for the suffering.

_____

_____

_____

_____

(i) Reach a judgement a

Having defined the key term and established a series of criteria, you should now make a judgement. Consider how far the black farmers suffered largely because of the actions of powerful landowners according to each criterion. Summarise your judgements below:

Criterion 1:

_____

Criterion 2:

_____

Criterion 3:

_____

Finally, sum up your judgement. Based on the criteria, how accurate is it to say that Southern black farmers suffered largely because of the actions of powerful landowners?

_____

_____

_____

_____

Tip: remember you should weigh up evidence of the landowners' actions against pre-Depression problems in agriculture and evidence of AAA policies and administration in your conclusion.

The impact of the New Deal, part 2

Segregation in the CCC

The Civilian Conservation Corps (CCC) was established in March 1933 in order to create jobs for the unemployed. The federal government recruited 17–24 (later 28) year-old unemployed males. Around 250,000 worked on reforestation, soil conservation and forest management projects in 1933–34, and 500,000 in 1935.

The CCC was headed by the racially conservative Tennesseean Robert Fechner. He was unenthusiastic about black workers, but in 1935 the Roosevelt administration ordered him to increase black recruitment.

Around 200,000 black Americans worked for the CCC during its nine–year existence, but

- they were usually restricted to lower–skilled jobs
- Fechner ordered 'complete segregation' of black and white workers in July 1935
- local whites often complained about having black recruits in their neighbourhood, e.g. in upstate New York and in Ohio
- white officials were frequently discriminatory, e.g. black recruits at Fort Dix, New Jersey, complained that they were evicted from their barracks to accommodate incoming white recruits, and that the officials refused to employ black clerks on the grounds that they were insufficiently intelligent.

However, some black Americans were impressed with the CCC. For example, New Yorker Luther Wandell wrote an article in the NAACP magazine *The Crisis* in 1935, saying that on balance, he had found employment in the CCC gratifying rather than disappointing.

Differential wages in the NRA

The National Recovery Administration (NRA) was set up in June 1933 to assist the recovery of businesses and manufacturing. Companies that adopted the codes that encouraged a minimum wage and maximum hours for workers were rewarded with the government's blue eagle symbol.

Black Americans did not benefit greatly from the NRA, however:

- The NRA allowed regionally differentiated wages, so that black workers' wages in the South were frequently unfairly low.
- The NRA excluded workers in agriculture and domestic service, and three-quarters of black Americans were employed in these areas. This was not an act of deliberate discrimination – it was due to the temporary nature of many jobs in these sectors.
- Employers often redefined black workers' jobs so as to avoid the set wage levels.

Black workers made jokes about what NRA stood for, e.g. Negroes Roasted Again, Negroes Rarely Allowed. However, some of the alphabet agencies were very helpful to black Americans, e.g. the National Youth Administration (NYA), in which black educator Mary McLeod Bethune was NYA Director of the Division of Negro affairs. The NYA gave aid and taught skills to 500,000 young black Americans and distributed money without regard to race, although it did accept segregation.

⚡ Develop the detail

Below is a sample exam-style question and a paragraph written in answer to this question. The paragraph contains a limited amount of detail. Annotate the paragraph to add additional detail to the answer.

How successful was the CCC in creating jobs for black Americans?

The CCC employed around 250,000 men in 1933–34 and 500,000 in 1935. It was headed by a racial conservative who was unenthusiastic about the capacities of black recruits and a believer in segregation. Some CCC officials at local level were also discriminatory. Furthermore, when black CCC recruits were sent to rural areas, the local white population often complained about their presence. However, some black Americans were grateful that the CCC offered them the opportunity to work.

⚡ Eliminate irrelevance a

Below is a sample exam-style question and a paragraph written in answer to this question. Read the paragraph and identify parts of the paragraph that are not directly relevant to the question. Draw a line through the information that is irrelevant and justify your deletions in the margin.

How accurate is it to say that the NRA was of little help to black Americans?

Companies that adopted the NRA codes that encouraged a minimum wage and maximum hours for workers were rewarded with the government's blue eagle symbol. However, black Americans did not benefit greatly from the NRA because the NRA allowed regionally differentiated wages, so that black workers' wages in the South were frequently unfairly low. The NRA excluded workers in agriculture and domestic service, and three-quarters of black Americans were employed in these areas. This was not an act of deliberate discrimination — it was due to the temporary nature of many jobs in these sectors. Employers often redefined black workers' jobs so as to avoid the set wage levels. On the other hand, some of the alphabet agencies were very helpful to black Americans. This was especially the case with the National Youth Administration (NYA), in which black educator Mary McLeod Bethune was NYA Director of the Division of Negro affairs. Bethune had an excellent working relationship with Eleanor Roosevelt and was a member of the so-called 'Black Cabinet'. The NYA gave aid and taught skills to 500,000 young black Americans and distributed money without regard to race, although it did accept segregation.

The impact of the New Deal, part 3

Benefits of welfare to black workers and their families

American attitudes to the role of government in welfare payments changed during the Depression.

The Federal Emergency Relief Administration (FERA)

FERA was established in May 1933. It spent over $4 billion to help the unemployed through relief and work projects. FERA was both advantageous and disadvantageous to black Americans:

Black Advantages	Black Disadvantages
Before the New Deal, state and local welfare agencies had usually ignored black needs, but one-third of black Americans were aided by FERA.	The distribution of FERA relief was often discriminatory at local level. Southern white officials made it harder for unemployed black Southerners to get on the welfare rolls and paid black welfare recipients less than whites, arguing that they were accustomed to a lower standard of living, e.g. in Atlanta, monthly relief cheques for whites were $32.66, but $19.29 for blacks. In some Georgia and Mississippi rural areas, black relief payments were 30 per cent lower than those of whites.

Social Security Act (August 1938)

This legislation set up insurance and pension schemes, to be funded by employer and employee contributions. It also established aid programmes for the physically disadvantaged and for families with dependent children.

The payments were low and did not kick in until 1940. The amount paid to families with dependent children varied according to the states – Mississippi only paid $8. There were further disadvantages for black Americans in particular. Many black Americans were waiters, waitresses, cooks, janitors and domestic and farm workers, and while these were probably the workers most in need of aid, they were excluded from Social Security coverage. Once again, this omission was due to the frequently temporary nature of employment in those areas rather than to racial discrimination.

Overall, the significance of welfare during the New Deal was that it reinforced the idea that black Americans should benefit from racially inclusive (if not racially equal) government programmes. That was a dramatic change from the years before Roosevelt and the Great Depression.

Impact on voting patterns

The role of Republican politicians in the Civil War and Reconstruction eras caused most black Americans to vote Republican. However, the New Deal triggered a black voting revolution.

While few Southern blacks could vote, there were significant numbers of Northern black voters and they switched their political allegiance from the Republicans to the Democrats during the 1930s. In 1932, around 70 per cent of black voters supported Republican presidential candidate Herbert Hoover, but in 1936, 76 per cent declared support for Roosevelt. In 1936, 1940 and 1944, most black voters voted for the Democrat Roosevelt. In 1940, he won 85 per cent of the votes in New York City's black Harlem ghetto.

Black Americans switched from Republican to Democrat because:

- Roosevelt and the Democrats were aware of the growing importance of the black vote in electorally pivotal states such as New York and Illinois. In 1936, Roosevelt promised 'no forgotten races' in a speech to a black audience and the Democratic Party showed its appreciation of the black vote when one of the 30 black delegates to the 1936 Democrat National Convention was given the honour of delivering the opening address
- many benefited from New Deal measures
- President Roosevelt dramatically increased the number of black federal employees from 50,000 in 1932 to 150,000 in 1941. Over 100 black Americans held significant administrative posts in New Deal agencies. There was even talk of a 'Black Cabinet' (a group of leading black New Dealers who frequently met the president)
- many believed that Franklin Roosevelt and, in particular, Eleanor Roosevelt, genuinely cared about them.

Qualify your judgement

Below is a sample exam-style question with an accompanying source. Having read the question and the source, complete the following activity.

Assess the usefulness of the Tennessee Valley Authority (TVA) to black Americans. Explain your answer, using the source, the information given about its origin and your own knowledge about the historical context.

Below are three judgements about the value of Source 1 to a historian investigating the usefulness of the TVA to black Americans. Circle the judgement that best describes the value of the source, and explain why it is the best.

1 Source 1 is valuable to a historian investigating the usefulness of the TVA to black Americans because the writer is a black man who might well have been an eyewitness to the TVA projects.

2 Source 1 is unreliable to a historian because it is biased.

3 Source 1 is partially valuable to historian investigating the usefulness of the TVA to black Americans, because it demonstrates the way in which the TVA officials discriminated against them. However, Source 1 is not wholly useful because it only describes the way in which the TVA discriminates. The source is limited as it does not emphasise that at the very least the TVA was employing and housing black workers.

SOURCE 1

The Tennessee Valley Authority (TVA) was a New Deal programme established in 1933. It constructed dams to control flooding and generated electricity. Information about the treatment of black workers was leaked to the NAACP by J. Max Bond, the TVA's black Supervisor of Negro Training. The result was an article by John Davis in The Crisis, *the NAACP's official news publication, on 1 October 1935. The article prompted a congressional committee to call for the improved treatment of black workers, after which the TVA proceeded a little more carefully. This is an extract from the article.*

… on TVA projects … Negroes were not employed in proportion to their numbers in the population and … received even less consideration in the matter of wage payments …

At Wilson Dam, Negroes are employed primarily in unskilled work … By reserving such occupations for Negroes, TVA effectively establishes a Negro differential, while at the same time loudly proclaiming: 'No discrimination is made between the races with reference to wages paid or hours of work.' … What is true of jobs at Wilson Dam is more or less true on other projects of TVA. Negro workmen have also been the victim of mis-classification, doing skilled work while receiving pay as unskilled workers … The men testified they were afraid to complain because the experience of other Negro workers had been that complaints about false classification led to dismissal.

… The failure to include a fair proportion of Negroes in skilled work … as well makes almost certain the gradual elimination of Negroes from employment by TVA. This is true because unskilled work is only necessary in the early stages of the dam projects …

The housing accommodations furnished Negro workers by TVA are notoriously inferior to those given whites … At Pickwick, the Negro community is separated from that for the white workers by a deep ravine. Officials of TVA suggested the reason for the separation to be the need for keeping down racial outbreaks which 'would be occasioned if Negroes and whites live together.' … In addition at Pickwick Negroes can attend the white theatre, if they sit in a 'Jim-Crow' section …

We have the tragic picture of officials of the federal government, sworn to uphold the Constitution, teaching white citizens that Negroes are unfit to live in any but segregated communities …

Now what is the present plight of the Negro dwellers in the Valley? … Negroes in the area are especially the victims of inadequate relief, low wages, intolerable living conditions and complete lack of any type of labour organisation … For Negroes the introduction of cheaper electric rates into Lee County as result of the TVA power policy has meant nothing. Landlords … have not found it to their advantage to wire their Negro tenants' homes … Thus so far as TVA's electrification programme is concerned the Negro family is still in outer darkness …

The impact of the New Deal, part 4

The work of Eleanor Roosevelt

President Roosevelt was anxious not to alienate Southern Democrats. Their votes were important for the passage of New Deal legislation that Roosevelt considered essential for all Americans, including black Americans. He did not want to jeopardise that legislation by emphasising black civil rights. However, his wife Eleanor Roosevelt was far more idealistic and quite willing to annoy Southern Democrats and members of her husband's administration by making clear her position on black American status:

- She ensured that prominent black Americans regularly met her husband, e.g. NAACP leader Walter White.

- She regularly met and was photographed with black Americans, e.g. her friend, black educator Mary McLeod Bethune.

- She attended black functions.

- In 1938, she attended the biracial Southern Conference of Human Welfare (SCHW) in Birmingham, Alabama, and insisted upon sitting alongside black delegates. The meeting declared support for equality before the law, voter registration for the poor, and financial aid for black students.

- In 1936, she invited black singer Marian Anderson to sing at the White House and in 1939, she resigned from the prestigious Daughters of the American Revolution because the organisation refused to allow Marian Anderson to sing before an integrated audience at their hall in Washington DC. Eleanor Roosevelt explained her reasons in her 'My Day' column, which was published in newspapers across the nation and reached an audience of around four million Americans.

- In 1940 alone, she promoted National Sharecroppers Week and the National Committee to Abolish the Poll Tax.

- In the Second World War, she advertised her support for the black Tuskegee airmen, whose aerial prowess was doubted by whites.

Privately, Eleanor Roosevelt put pressure on her husband to endorse the Costigan–Wagner anti-lynching legislation and on New Deal officials to provide non-discriminatory aid, especially in the South. In 1941, she helped avert a threatened black March on Washington that aimed to protest against racial discrimination in the defence industries. This would have brought the nation's capital to a standstill in wartime. The First Lady met with black leaders then persuaded her husband to set up the Fair Employment Practices Commission (FEPC). The march was cancelled and a crisis averted.

Contemporary reactions to Eleanor Roosevelt

Many whites disliked Eleanor Roosevelt's stance on race. For example, she had defended the construction of an integrated housing development in Detroit and the integration led to a race riot. There was much press criticism of her role in this. One headline read, 'There is blood on your hands, Mrs Roosevelt'. The Southern press in particular loathed her, and suggested that she must have black blood – a sure sign that her sympathy for black Americans was well known and highly significant.

! Delete as applicable   a

Below are a sample exam-style question and a paragraph written in answer to this question. Read the paragraph and decide which of the possible options (in bold) is most appropriate. Delete the least appropriate options and complete the paragraph by justifying your selection.

'Eleanor Roosevelt contributed a great deal to black American advancement.'

How far do you agree with this statement??

> While President Roosevelt was anxious to avoid alienating Southern white Democrats, his wife made clear her sympathy for the black American situation in the South in particular. She contributed **a great deal/considerably/very little** to advances in black American status. She supported the 'Black Cabinet', arranged meetings between leading black Americans and her husband, and ostentatiously met with black Americans and attended black functions. She made it clear that she opposed the Jim Crow laws in Birmingham in 1938 and when she resigned her membership of the DAR in 1939. She also made it clear that she opposed political inequality (she campaigned against the poll tax) and that she rejected ideas of black intellectual inferiority (she supported the Tuskegee airmen). Overall, within the limitations of the First Lady's role, she made **a significant/ reasonably significant/insignificant contribution** to the idea that black Americans were unfairly treated because
>
> _____
>
> _____

↕ Identify key phrases   a

Below is a sample exam-style question that includes

- a key phrase relating to contents
- a key phrase relating to the evaluation required of you.

Key phrases are important because their meaning can be helpful in structuring your answer, developing an argument and establishing criteria that will help form the basis of a judgement.

> How accurate is it to say that Eleanor Roosevelt was the most important factor in changes in black voting allegiance?

First, identify the key phrase that focuses upon the content of the question.

Second, define that key phrase. Your definition should set out the key features of the phrase or word that you are defining.

Third, identify the key phrase that directs you to evaluation.

Fourth, make an essay plan that reflects these two key phrases.

Finally, write a sentence answering the question that refers back to your two key phrases.

Now repeat the task with the question below, and consider how the changing key terms affects the structure, argument and final judgement of your essay.

> To what extent did the actions of Eleanor Roosevelt impact upon black American status in the years 1933–41?

Exam focus

Below is a source, question and sample answer on the treatment of black Americans in the CCC and white attitudes to black recruits in the CCC.

Assess the value of the source for revealing black attitudes to the CCC and white attitudes to black Americans. Explain your answer, using the source, the information given about its origin and your own knowledge about the historical context.

SOURCE 1

From an article by a black American from New York, Luther C. Wandall, in the NAACP magazine The Crisis, *published in August 1935. Wandall applied for and obtained a position in the CCC.*

During the two years of its previous existence I had heard many conflicting reports concerning the Civilian Conservation Corps, President Roosevelt's pet project. One boy told me that he almost froze to death one night out in Washington. Some said that the colored got all the leftovers. Others said that everything was all right. But my brother, who is a World War veteran, advised me emphatically: 'I wouldn't be in anything connected with the Army.' So it was with some apprehension ... that I was 'accepted for enrollment'.

... We reached Camp Dix about 7:30 that evening ... here it was that Mr. James Crow first definitely put in his appearance ... until now there had been no distinction made. But before we left the bus the officer shouted emphatically: 'Colored boys fall out in the rear.' The colored from several buses were herded together, and stood in line until after the white boys had been registered and taken to their tents. This seemed to be the established order of procedure at Camp Dix.

This separation of the colored from the whites was completely and rigidly maintained at this camp ... I was interested to observe these officers ... Many of them were southerners, how many I could not tell. Out of their official character they were usually courteous, kindly, refined, and even intimate. They offered extra money to any of us who could sing or dance. On the other hand, some were vicious and ill-tempered, and apparently restrained only by fear ...

We were finally led away to our tents ... the worst in Camp Dix ... By now only one thought occupied my mind: When do I leave this place? ... So you can imagine my feelings when an officer, a small quiet fellow, obviously a southerner, asked me how I would like to stay in Camp Dix permanently as his clerk! This officer was very courteous, and seemed to be used to colored people, and liked them. I declined his offer ... Food at Camp Dix was poor in quality and variety, and barely sufficient in quantity ... We stayed at Camp Dix eight days.

We were taken to permanent camp in the upper South. This camp was a dream compared with Camp Dix. There was plenty to eat, and we slept in barracks instead of tents. An excellent recreation hall, playground, and other facilities. ... Our bosses are local men, southerners, but on the whole I have found nothing to complain of. The work varies, but is always healthy, outdoor labor ... Our officers, who, of course, are white, are a captain, a first lieutenant, a doctor, and several sergeants. Our athletic director is colored, as is our vocational teacher ... On the whole, I was gratified rather than disappointed with the CCC. I had expected the worst. Of course it reflects, to some extent, all the practices and prejudices of the US Army. But as a job and an experience, for a man who has no work, I can heartily recommend it.

This source is a first-hand account of the experiences of one rather unusual black American in the CCC. It is valuable for revealing the attitudes of some black Americans toward the CCC and of some white Americans toward the black recruits, although the unusual character of the writer and the place of publication need particular consideration.

Luther Wandell had heard 'conflicting reports' from fellow black Americans about life in the CCC. One boy 'almost froze to death' in it, and some said black recruits 'got all the leftovers'. A great deal of contemporary evidence confirms discriminatory practice in the CCC, as shown in the Norfolk Journal and Guide's account of the firing of Eddie Simons from the CCC camp at North Lisbon, New Jersey, in 1934. This was unsurprising as the CCC was run by the conservative Tennessean Robert Fechner, who had a low opinion of black workers. Army officers ran CCC camps, and Wandell's brother, who had experienced the segregation in the Armed Forces in the First World War, advised against enrolment in the CCC. The source is a valuable reminder that many black Americans had a hostile attitude to the CCC and the segregation that Wandell experienced helps explain that attitude – he met with 'Mr James Crow' from the first, even in Camp Dix in the Northern state of New Jersey.

However, Wandell himself found 'nothing to complain of' and much to be satisfied with in his 'permanent camp in the South'. He was generally 'gratified rather than disappointed' with his employment in the CCC and had a tolerant attitude toward the CCC, despite its reflection of the segregationist 'practice and prejudices' of the US Army. He recognised that 'as a job and an experience' for the unemployed, it was extremely helpful – he can 'heartily recommend it'. This seems like a balanced and therefore useful account of black attitudes to the CCC. Judging from Wandell's friends and family, black attitudes were generally hostile, and Wandell seems exceptional in his more positive attitude. Wandell might of course have been atypical. He seems to have been a particularly literate and thoughtful individual – not many people, black or white, had articles published in a magazine, and given the generally lower standard of black education, Wandell was quite unusual. The fact that the NAACP, which was always so quick to point out and publicise unequal treatment of black Americans, published Wandell's account suggests that on balance, Wandell was not the only black American with a generally positive attitude toward the opportunities offered by the CCC, even if it was segregationist. It is possible that black attitudes to the CCC were so hostile as to be counter-productive – black Americans needed jobs and the CCC provided them, so that the NAACP, which was always ready to be critical of New Deal agencies, might have felt that it needed to redress the balance in Crisis.

This introduction is quite effective, because it focuses upon the question and indicates that the source needs to be treated with caution.

This paragraph covers hostile black American attitudes to the CCC, provides appropriate quotations from the passage and refers back to the question. It also supports the source with background knowledge.

This paragraph covers more positive attitudes to the CCC, but it introduces a tone of caution by considering the provenance and asking whether Wandell was atypical and whether the NAACP was attempting to demonstrate more balanced attitudes than was usual.

The source is also balanced in its coverage of white American attitudes toward black recruits. It is a useful reminder that segregation was not confined to the South. The segregation at Fort Dix was due to the Army's segregation policies and Wandell came from *de facto* segregated Harlem. Segregation, whether *de facto* or *de jure*, reflected nationwide racist white American attitudes. Such attitudes were not simply a Southern phenomenon. Interestingly, Wandell notes that some Southern officers were 'usually courteous ... even intimate'. However, it might be unwitting testimony to the patronising attitude of many Southern whites to black Americans when Wandell notes that the Southern officers offered money 'to any of us who could sing or dance'. The implication there is that the Southerners felt black Americans had a particular aptitude for giving, and a desire to give, entertainment to whites. One wonders whether Wandell was recounting this tongue in cheek, because he quickly moves on to his own experience as if to reassure us that he was something more than a song and dance man. Wandell tells of the Southern white officer who offered him a clerkship at Fort Dix, clearly considering him capable of working at a higher level than the usual black manual labourer. This officer 'liked' black Americans. Clearly, Wandell experienced both positive and negative white attitudes: while some white CCC officials were pleasant, others were 'vicious and ill-tempered'.

Along with some positive and some negative attitudes on the part of white Americans toward Wandell personally, he tells us how, although the officers are white 'of course', there are two black Americans in positions of some responsibility: the 'athletic director' and the 'vocational teacher'. However, these are 'our' officials, so it may be that those two were only dealing with the black recruits and, by implication, unfit to deal with white recruits. Overall, it seems that for the most part the white attitude toward black recruits in the CCC is that although they should be treated carefully, they cannot cope with or are unworthy of positions of great responsibility. Even President Roosevelt shared this attitude. In September 1935, he sent a brief handwritten letter to Robert Fechner asking him to 'please try to put in colored foremen, not of course in technical work but in the ordinary manual work'.

Overall then, the source is valuable in reminding us of the varied black attitudes of black people toward the CCC and of white Americans to black Americans. In giving the impression of varying attitudes and complex interracial relationships, it seems to reflect the contemporary situation accurately. In 1938, Mary McLeod Bethune told an audience of black educators, 'We are scorned of men; they spit in our faces and laugh', and yet in 1936, 1940 and in 1944, the majority of black voters supported Franklin Roosevelt. The source is a useful and accurate reflection of how contemporary race relations were in a state of flux – 'We ain't what we ought to be ... But thank God Almighty, we ain't what we used to be.'

This paragraph moves on to the second enquiry. It explores positive and negative white American attitudes to black Americans.

This paragraph looks at the issue of black Americans in positions of responsibility in the CCC. It integrates the content of the source with confirmatory background knowledge about Roosevelt's attitude.

This is a good answer. The candidate engages with the question and analyses the source material. The answer would be even better if the candidate was more explicit in evaluating the usefulness of the source. It is a good idea to signpost to the examiner at the end of each paragraph a mini conclusion about the usefulness of the source.

Reverse engineering

Read the essay and the comments and try to work out the general points of the plan used to write the essay. Once you have done this, note down the specific examples used to support each general point.

4 'I have a dream', 1954–68

Civil rights activities, 1954–63

In 1954, the most notable civil rights activists were the leaders and lawyers of the NAACP, financed by tens of thousands of members nationwide. NAACP activism focused upon the erosion of Plessy v. Ferguson in the nation's law courts. The Supreme Court supported the South's Jim Crow laws in the late nineteenth century, but changed its position in the twentieth century. The most important Supreme Court ruling against segregation was the Brown v. Board of Education ruling in 1954.

The role of Earl Warren and the Supreme Court

Several black litigants, including Oliver Brown, sought NAACP aid in opposing segregated schools. Leading NAACP lawyer **Thurgood Marshall** argued that segregation was against the 14th Amendment and the Supreme Court ruled that even if school facilities were equal (they never were), segregation was psychologically harmful to black children.

The role of **Earl Warren** had been:

- **vital**. He worked long, hard and successfully for consensus amongst the nine Supreme Court justices on Brown, believing their unanimity would help gain support for desegregation.
- **controversial**. President **Eisenhower** had appointed Warren and told him to oppose integrated schools. When Warren ignored him, Eisenhower described Warren's appointment as his 'biggest damn fool mistake' ever.
- **realistic**. The court gave no date for the completion of desegregation, not even in Brown II (1955), because Warren rightly anticipated that schools and administrators needed time to adjust.

The role of the Supreme Court had been:

- **inspirational**. Rosa Parks noted how the Brown ruling inspired further activism.
- **influential**. Brown seemed to remove all constitutional sanctions for Plessy v. Ferguson, and some schools in urban areas (e.g. Washington DC) and border states (e.g. Maryland) desegregated, although there was resistance (the Supreme Court had no powers of enforcement).

- **controversial**. The ruling inspired the establishment of White Citizens' Councils across the South. They aimed to defend segregation and boasted 250,000 members by 1956. The Ku Klux Klan was revitalised. The most famous white resistance was at Central High School, in Little Rock, Arkansas, where a white mob tried to exclude nine black students, and Eisenhower had to send in federal forces.

The impact of victory in Montgomery

In December 1955, Rosa Parks was arrested for refusing to give up her seat to a white man on a segregated Montgomery, Alabama, bus. Montgomery's black community boycotted the buses for a year until the NAACP won a Supreme Court ruling against segregated buses in Browder v. Gayle.

Victory in Montgomery had a dramatic impact:

- The boycott had continued despite opposition from Montgomery's White Citizens' Council and the harassment of black activists. This boosted black Southerners' morale and inspired more resistance.
- The desegregation was very much an NAACP victory, but the commitment and bravery of Montgomery's black community encouraged further black direct, non-violent action.
- The choice of Martin Luther King as leader of the Montgomery Improvement Association brought him to national attention. He set up the Southern Christian Leadership Conference (SCLC) in 1957, but it achieved little at first.
- Montgomery businesses lost $1 million when the black population could not access the downtown shops so easily. This encouraged some Southern white business owners to oppose segregation.
- In Montgomery itself, the impact was limited. Only the buses were desegregated.
- The boycott inspired similar successful boycotts in 20 other Southern cities.
- The boycott inspired individuals (e.g. Melba Pattillo, one of the Little Rock Nine) and Northern white support for Southern black activism.

Quick quizzes at **www.hoddereducation.co.uk/myrevisionnotes**

Moving from assertion to argument

Below are a sample exam-style question and a series of assertions. Read the exam question and then add a justification to each of the assertions to turn it into an argument.

How significant was the role of the Supreme Court in civil rights in the years 1954–63?

The Supreme Court's position on black rights changed dramatically between the 1880s and 1950s, as attested by

_____

_____

The Brown ruling did not transform education in the South because

_____

_____

Eisenhower obviously thought the Brown ruling owed everything to Earl Warren, because

_____

_____

Browder v. Gayle was of limited significance to Montgomery because

_____

_____

The flaw in the argument

Below are a sample exam-style question and a paragraph written in answer to the question. The paragraph contains an argument which attempts to answer the question. However, there is an error in the argument. Use your knowledge of this topic to identify the flaw in the argument.

How accurate is it to say that Martin Luther King was responsible for the ending of segregated buses in Montgomery in 1956?

Martin Luther King was mainly responsible for ending segregation on Montgomery's buses through his leadership of the Montgomery Improvement Association. His rhetorical talents gained him national attention and considerable praise and without him the boycott would not have been successful. Montgomery's black community gave near total support to the boycott, and after NAACP litigation won the Browder v. Gayle ruling in 1956, the buses were desegregated.

The work and impact of Martin Luther King, SCLC, SNCC and CORE, 1957–63

Four years after the Montgomery bus boycott, students kick-started the civil rights movement.

Sit-ins and SNCC, 1960

In 1960, four black college students refused to leave their seats at the Woolworth's segregated lunch counter in Greensboro, North Carolina. Other students relieved them and the lunch counter had to close. Such sit-ins spread across the South.

The impact of the sit-ins was great:

- Woolworth's desegregated their lunch counters across the South by the end of 1961.
- 150 Southern cities desegregated some public places.
- Direct action had clearly replaced litigation as the favourite mode of black activists.
- 70,000 students participated in sit-ins across the South, suggesting that a real civil rights movement had begun.
- The students set up their own organisation – the **Student Non-Violent Coordinating Committee (SNCC)**.
- SNCC worked to empower and mobilise ordinary black Americans in several areas, notably in a black voter registration campaign in the Mississippi Delta.
- These were the first sit-ins to attract nationwide media coverage and attention.

CORE and the Freedom Rides, 1961

The **Congress of Racial Equality (CORE)** was established by James Farmer in Chicago in 1942. It organised sit-ins in segregated Chicago eateries during the war and tested the Supreme Court's Morgan v. Virginia ruling in 1947. In 1961, CORE promoted integrated student group bus rides across the South to test the Supreme Court's ruling in Boynton v. Virginia (1960) against segregated interstate bus facilities.

These **'Freedom Rides'** had a great impact:

- They demonstrated the enthusiastic and brave activism of the younger black generation.
- White racist attacks on the buses, especially at Anniston, Alabama, publicised the lawlessness of Southern whites, as Farmer had hoped.
- The violence persuaded Attorney General Robert Kennedy to try to enforce Supreme Court rulings against segregated interstate transport.

Martin Luther King, SCLC and Birmingham

King and SCLC had tried working at grassroots level with a Crusade for Citizenship, but this voter registration campaign was poorly funded and understaffed. King decided that brief, attention-grabbing campaigns were more effective work.

In 1963, King orchestrated marches in Birmingham, Alabama, because he knew that police chief Bull Connor would react violently and gain publicity that might persuade President **John F. Kennedy** to promote the civil rights bill.

King's Birmingham campaign had a great impact:

- Connor's dogs and fire hoses, police mistreatment of young protesters and Birmingham's overflowing jails were all headline news. President Kennedy admitted that the Southern situation was intolerable and promoted the civil rights bill more enthusiastically.
- King and SCLC had worked successfully for the first time.

The March on Washington, 1963

The March on Washington was masterminded by black trade union leader **A. Philip Randolph**, who sought passage of the civil rights bill and more black employment opportunities. All the major black organisations participated.

The nationally televised March on Washington had a considerable impact:

- The well-behaved, integrated crowd of 250,000 made a good impression nationwide.
- Some people believe the March encouraged Congress to pass the civil rights bill.
- King's 'I have a dream' speech was the inspirational highlight. It called upon white Americans to live up to the words and principles of their beloved Declaration of Independence, Constitution and Christian beliefs.

Select the detail

Below is an exam-style question with the accompanying source and three claims that you could make when answering the question. Read the claims and then select quotes from the source to support them. Remember to keep the quotes short as sometimes a few words embedded in a sentence are all you need to support your claims.

Assess the value of the source for revealing the motives of the Freedom Riders and white attitudes to black Americans.

Some Freedom Riders were motivated primarily because of a deeply personal sense of injustice.

_____

_____

Some Freedom Riders were motivated by religion.

_____

_____

The 1960s was a decade of protest and this inspired some of the Freedom Riders.

_____

_____

_____

SOURCE 1

Extracts from transcripts of interviews with Freedom Riders (no date given), quoted on www.outreach.olemiss. edu/Freedom_Riders/Resources/

1. Charles Person, African American: I grew up in Atlanta ... at a time when America needed scientists ... My [test] scores and my [grades] were good enough to get me accepted at MIT [Massachusetts Institute of Technology], but Georgia Tech was also the number one engineering school in the South, so I applied to Georgia Tech, and of course rejected my application. So I could not understand, here we were competing with the Russians, because the Russians had launched Sputnik, and we say we needed scientists, yet I was being denied an opportunity to go to a school which I was eminently qualified to go to, so that gave me the impetus to get involved in all the civil rights activities that were happening on campus ... So this was a great time, the energy on campus with all the kids being involved in all those kind of activities, it just snowballed. Once I got involved, it was infectious.

2. Sandra Nixon, African American: I grew up in New Orleans ... I was ... in college at Southern University in New Orleans and met some ... members of the Congress on Racial Equality. After listening to them talking about the social injustices that were going on in the city of New Orleans, I decided to become a member of ... CORE.

3. Joan Trumpower Mulholland, white: I was born in Washington DC ... My involvement came about from my religious conviction, and the contradiction between life in America with what was being taught in Sunday School. I was at Duke University in Durham [North Carolina], which was the second city to have sit-ins, and the Presbyterian chaplain arranged for the students ... to come over and talk with us about what the sit-ins were about and the philosophical and religious underpinnings ... At the end, they invited us to join them on sit-ins in the next week or so, and that started a snowball effect.

4. Albert Gordon, white: Why some of us have been ready to do things, and others not? In my own past, I was born in Europe, and I did see the Nazis, and most of my family was killed by the Nazis during World War II in the concentration camp, because I was Jewish ... So those things can explain in part my social conscience, but by no means all together ... When I saw the young people first in the first sit-ins and the courage that they had to have, and then saw a couple of years later the bus in Anniston, and Jim Peck being so brutally beaten, I thought I just had to do something, and simply volunteered and proceeded.

Civil rights legislation in the 1960s

During the 1960s, two major civil rights bills were passed: the 1964 Civil Rights Act and the 1965 Voting Rights Act. A third Act, the 1968 Civil Rights Act (the Fair Housing Act), was far less effective. Black activism, white public opinion, Congress and President **Lyndon Johnson** all played an important part in this legislation.

The importance of the Civil Rights Act (1964)

Several factors explain the passage of the 1964 Civil Rights Act:

- Black activism exposed Southern white racism to the world, e.g. Birmingham, and convinced some white Americans to try to live up to their professed ideals, e.g. March on Washington.
- White opinion was changing (by January 1964, 68 per cent of Americans favoured the bill) and Congress responded to that.
- President Kennedy had won over the Republican minority leader to the bill.
- When President Kennedy was assassinated (November 1963), some members of Congress considered passage of the bill a fitting tribute to him.
- President Johnson worked hard to get the bill passed.

The 1964 Civil Rights Act was important because it

- prohibited discrimination in public places (Jim Crow segregation laws were illegal)
- furthered school desegregation
- gave the federal government the legal tools to end *de jure* segregation in the South
- established an Equal Employment Commission
- helped revolutionise the South.

But although it was a giant step forward for black Americans in the South, problems remained because

- the 1964 Act did nothing to promote black voting in the South
- it did nothing about the poverty and discrimination suffered by black Americans in the big city ghettos outside the South, e.g. Harlem in New York City, the South Side in Chicago and Watts in Los Angeles.

The importance of the Voting Rights Act (1965)

The Voting Rights Act of 1965 was passed because:

- the Civil Rights Act had not helped would-be black voters to get registered in the face of Southern white registrars who closed their office door to black people or set them impossible literacy tests, e.g. half of the population of Selma, Alabama, was black but only 23 of them had been able to register to vote.
- Martin Luther King's 1965 Selma campaign exposed Southern white racism and brutality, e.g. TV viewers saw state troopers attack marchers with clubs and tear gas on 'Bloody Sunday', which aroused nationwide condemnation of Southern white behaviour.

The Voting Rights Act provided for federally appointed registrars to combat Southern white devices such as literacy tests. The importance of the Act was that

- it revolutionised Southern politics
- by late 1966, only four of the old Confederate states had fewer than 50 per cent of eligible black voters registered; by 1968, even Mississippi was up to 59 per cent
- the number of black Americans elected to office in the South increased sixfold between 1965 and 1969. This facilitated the passage of legislation in the US Congress and in state legislatures that had a positive effect on black American lives, but also restrained the passage of legislation that would have had an adverse impact.

! Mind map

Use the information on the page opposite to add detail to the mind map below to show the reasons why civil rights legislation was passed in 1964–65.

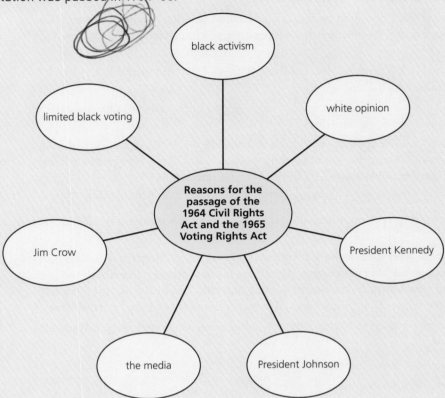

i Developing an argument   a

Below is a sample exam-style question on the reasons for the civil rights legislation of 1964–65, a list of key points to be made in a paragraph on King's contribution and a version of that paragraph. Read the question, the plan and the sample paragraph. Rewrite the paragraph in order to develop an argument. Your paragraph should answer the question directly and set out the evidence that supports your argument. Crucially, it should develop an argument by setting out a general answer to the question and reasons that support this.

How accurate is it to say that black activism was responsible for the passage of the civil rights legislation of 1964–65?

Key points:

- King's Birmingham campaign in 1963 exposed Southern white racism to the world.
- King's speech during the March on Washington in 1963 inspired many white Americans to live up to their declared ideals and beliefs.
- King's Selma campaign in 1965 further exposed Southern white racism.

King's Birmingham campaign in 1963 exposed Southern white racism to the world. The media showed Bull Connor's use of police dogs and fire hoses against black children as young as six years old. Soon after, King's 'I have a dream' speech during the March on Washington inspired many white Americans to live up to their declared ideals and beliefs. He referred to the Declaration of Independence, the Constitution and the Bible. He had a third great success at Selma in 1965, where his campaign exposed Southern white racism, notably on Bloody Sunday.

The importance of the 1968 Civil Rights Act

After the Voting Rights Act of 1965, President Johnson found it difficult to persuade Congress to pass more legislation to help black Americans because:

- outbreaks of costly black rioting in protest against ghetto conditions in the North and West in each of the summers of 1964–68 alienated white voters and Congress, e.g. Watts, Los Angeles, 1965
- from 1966, many black Americans rejected King's non-violence and turned to the **Black Power movement**, which alienated whites
- white voters did not want tax rises to finance costly ghetto improvements, especially when the Vietnam War was increasingly expensive
- Congress reflected white exasperation with black demands, e.g. in 1966, it rejected a Johnson civil rights bill to end discrimination in housing (polls revealed that 70 per cent of whites opposed large numbers of black residents in their neighbourhoods).

In 1968, Congress passed a Civil Rights Act because:

- Johnson continued to press Congress to do something about discrimination in sales and rental of housing
- white homeowners, banks and realtors (estate agents) generally cooperated in excluding black Americans from moving into white areas, e.g. whites in the working-class suburb of Cicero in Chicago opposed black families moving in because of racism and/or the fact that property values went down when black families moved in (other whites would then avoid the area)
- the spring 1968 assassination of Martin Luther King generated a guilty feeling that something ought to be done.

The 1968 Civil Rights Act was important because it

- tried to prohibit discrimination in sales and rentals
- proved ineffective in practice because of white opposition
- demonstrated that racism could not be legislated out of existence and that Congress and white Americans had lost interest in further promotion of black equality (the executive and the judiciary took up the battle through the promotion of **affirmative action**).

The role of Lyndon Johnson

Although a Southerner, Johnson genuinely sought to help black Americans because he:

- considered America sufficiently rich and liberal to create a 'Great Society' in which poverty and racism were eradicated
- believed greater black equality would help revitalise the South, one of the poorest regions in the nation
- feared continuing racial inequality could lead to violence.

Johnson played a crucial role in the passage of the 1964 Civil Rights Act:

- he made emotive appeals to President Kennedy's memory and to national traditions
- he expended a massive amount of time, energy and political capital in breaking the Southern filibuster
- he won over some Southerners by appealing to their self-interest, e.g. he promised them federal expenditure in their area.

Those methods were subsequently unsuccessful. It took King's Selma campaign and Bloody Sunday to get the 1965 Voting Rights Act through Congress, and Martin Luther King's assassination to get the 1968 Civil Rights Act.

! Simple essay style   a

Below is a sample exam-style question. Use your own knowledge and the information on the opposite page to produce a plan for this question. Choose four general points, and provide three pieces of specific information to support each general point. Once you have planned your essay, write the introduction and conclusion for the essay. The introduction should list the points to be discussed in the essay. The conclusion should summarise the key points and justify which point was the most important.

How accurate is it to say that the civil rights legislation in 1964, 1965 and 1968 was primarily the work of Lyndon Johnson?

! Support or challenge?   a

Below is a sample exam-style question which asks you to what extent you agree with a specific statement. Below that is a list of general statements which are relevant to the question. Using your own knowledge and the information on the opposite page, decide whether these statements support or challenge the statement in question.

'The civil rights legislation of 1964–68 achieved little.' How far do you agree with this statement?

STATEMENT	SUPPORT	CHALLENGE
White homeowners, bankers and realtors ignored the 1968 Civil Rights Act.		
After the 1965 Voting Rights Act, the number of black legislators was still not in proportion to the percentage of black citizens.		
The annual and widespread ghetto riots of 1964–68 demonstrated continued black economic and social inequality.		
De jure segregation was illegal after 1964.		
After the 1965 Voting Rights Act, the number of elected black officials in the South increased six times over.		
The 1964 Civil Rights Act did nothing to combat literacy tests.		

Increasing divisions, part 1

The increasing divisions over black rights in the second half of the 1960s were well illustrated by the life and career of Malcolm X.

The role of Malcom X

The **Nation of Islam (NOI)** was a separatist black nationalist religion established in 1930 in Detroit's black ghetto. Membership grew dramatically in the 1950s because ghetto inhabitants felt better when Malcolm's preaching and the NOI:

● emphasised working to improve ghetto life

● taught that the evil scientist Yacub created the evil white race but that black people would ultimately rule the world under Allah

● transformed white-imposed *de facto* segregation into something positive by advocating separatism

● rejected the white man's Christian religion and provided an alternative religion for black people

● encouraged followers to behave in a self-disciplined way that helped restore black pride and morale.

The role of Malcolm X was:

● inspirational in the ghettos – during the 1950s Malcolm's preaching attracted thousands of new members into the NOI; his autobiography comforted other black Americans whom whites had traditionally made feel inferior

● inspirational in the black activist movement – he influenced the younger generation of black activists (e.g. **Stokely Carmichael** and the Black Power movement)

● controversial – white Americans felt he incited violence when he said that black people could advance 'by any means necessary'

● negative – he criticised King's methods and he alienated whites

● provocative – he encouraged critical thinking about America's race problems, claiming that he reminded the white man of the alternative to Dr King

● divisive – Malcolm alienated whites, criticised King's integrationism as demeaning and eventually condemned the NOI (he disagreed with NOI leader Elijah Muhammad's womanising and rejection of political involvement)

● inconsistent – after leaving the NOI, Malcolm claimed he had repudiated its racist theology.

The expulsion of whites from SNCC and CORE

James Meredith, the first black student at the University of Mississippi, undertook a March from Memphis, Tennessee, to Jackson, Mississippi, in 1966 with the aim of encouraging black voting. When he got shot and was hospitalised, SCLC and SNCC continued his march.

The Meredith March exposed black divisions:

● The NAACP dropped out when SNCC leader Stokely Carmichael criticised the new civil rights bill.

● SNCC opposed white marchers, while King favoured an integrated march.

● SNCC followers chanted 'Black Power', and King's followers responded with 'Freedom Now'.

● King despaired of SNCC.

The Meredith March demonstrated the radicalisation of SNCC, which was caused by

● impatience with the slow progress toward black equality

● disillusionment with the lack of federal protection during SNCC's Freedom Summer voter registration campaign in Mississippi in 1964

● the feeling that King and the civil rights movement had proved inattentive and ineffective over ghetto problems.

CORE was also radicalised because of slow progress and ghetto problems:

● *de facto* segregated housing was poor and black Americans struggled to move out (whites would not sell/rent to them)

● schools were poor and only 32 per cent completed high school (compared to 56 per cent for whites)

● economic opportunities were limited due to poor education, poverty and increasing automation, e.g. Chicago's ghetto had 50–70 per cent black youth unemployment.

In 1966, CORE endorsed Black Power and declared non-violence inappropriate. By 1968, CORE and SNCC excluded white members. In 1968, SNCC merged with the **Black Panthers**.

(!) Spot the mistake

Below is a sample exam-style question and a paragraph written in answer to this question. Why does this paragraph not get high praise? What is wrong with the focus of the answer in this paragraph?

> How far do you agree that Malcolm X played a positive role for the black community in the 1960s?

> Malcolm X played an important role for the black community in the 1960s. He criticised Martin Luther King's methods and called him an 'Uncle Tom'. Ghetto residents found his preaching and his autobiography uplifting because he took pride in blackness. He inspired the younger generation, including SNCC's leader Stokely Carmichael, and the Black Power movement. He kept ghetto problems on the national political agenda.

( ) Support your judgement

Below is a sample exam-style question and two basic judgements. Read the exam question and the two judgements. Support the judgement that you agree with more strongly by adding a reason that justifies the judgement.

> How accurate is it to say that Malcolm X played a negative role in the advancement of black rights?

> Overall, Malcolm played a negative role in the advancement of black rights because he criticised King's methods and he alienated white Americans, but
>
> _____
>
> _____
>
> _____

> Generally, Malcolm played a positive role in the advancement of black rights, because he inspired the younger black generation and he frightened whites into acceptance of the demands made by Martin Luther King in Birmingham and Selma, although
>
> _____
>
> _____
>
> _____

Tip: whichever option you choose you will have to weigh up both sides of the argument. You could use words such as 'whereas' or 'although' in order to help the process of evaluation.

The growth of the Black Panthers

The Black Panthers were established in 1966 in Oakland, California, by Huey Newton and Bobby Seale. They advocated:

- full employment and better housing and education in the ghettos
- self-determination
- an end to police brutality
- appreciation of black culture and the teaching of black history.

Although the Black Panthers were big news, their organisation only ever gained around 5,000 members in local chapters in ghettos in cities such as Oakland, Boston, New Orleans and Chicago. Black Panther activities included

- practical aid for ghetto residents, e.g. 40 clinics advising on health, welfare and legal rights
- the provision of free breakfasts for thousands of black children
- the promotion of knowledge about black history and sickle cell anaemia
- the tailing of white police in order to expose police brutality.

They impressed young black Americans through their paramilitary uniform and their newsworthy exploits, e.g. they surrounded and entered the California state legislature to protest against repressive legislation. Polls showed that 64 per cent of black Americans were proud of the Black Panthers, but they were in decline by the early 1970s because they were targeted by the police and FBI.

The Black Panthers were the most famous group in the Black Power movement. The Black Power movement was hard to define. It meant different things to different people, including:

- black pride, e.g. in African culture
- black violence
- black separatism
- black supremacy
- black capitalism.

King's stance on the Vietnam War

After his Selma campaign triggered the Voting Rights Act, Martin Luther King:

- was derided as an Uncle Tom by many in the Black Power movement
- failed to bring about any improvements in the ghettos in his Chicago campaign of 1966
- gained little support for his attempt at a multiracial 'Poor People's Campaign' in 1968
- opposed the Vietnam War, which alienated black Americans who thought he should only focus upon civil rights, President Johnson and some white Americans.

King opposed US involvement in the Vietnam War because:

- there were a disproportionate number of black casualties (black soldiers were invariably sent to the front lines)
- the Vietnamese suffered poverty and racism just as black Americans did
- Vietnamese children were suffering greatly because of American weaponry
- the war diverted funds from Johnson's Great Society programmes, some of which had helped ghetto residents
- black soldiers were being sent to guarantee liberties in Southeast Asia while they suffered inequality and discrimination in the United States
- the government's use of violence as a solution to Communism in Vietnam made it difficult to condemn violence in the ghettos.

King's assassination and its immediate effects

In March 1968, King went to Memphis, Tennessee, to support striking black sanitation workers. He was assassinated by a white racist. The immediate effects were:

- nationwide ghetto riots
- Congress felt it had to pass the Civil Rights Act, which attempted to combat discrimination in housing.

⊹ RAG – Rate the timeline

Below is a sample exam-style question and a timeline. Read the question, study the timeline and using three coloured pens, put a red, amber or green star next to the events to show:

Red: events and policies that have no relevance to the question

Amber: events and policies that have some significance to the question

Green: events and policies that are directly relevant to the question

To what extent were black divisions due to Martin Luther King?

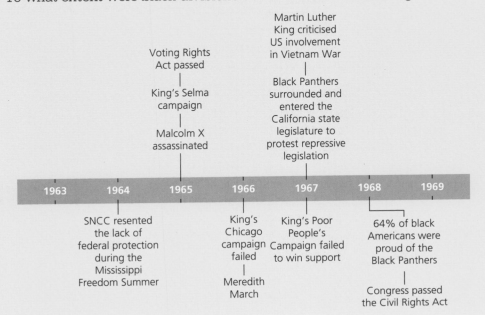

ⓘ Recommended reading

Below is a list of suggested further reading on this topic.

Adam Fairclough, *Better Day Coming: Blacks and Equality, 1890–2000* (2001).

David Garrow, *Bearing the Cross: Martin Luther King, Jr, and the Southern Christian Leadership Conference* (1999).

Manning Marable, *Malcolm X: A Life of Reinvention* (2011)

Exam focus

Below is a sample answer on the situation of black Americans, 1954–68.

To what extent did civil rights activists improve the lives of black Americans in the years 1954–68?

In the years 1954–68, federal government actions that improved black American lives included important Supreme Court rulings such as Brown v. Board of Education (1954) and Browder v. Gayle (1956), congressional legislation such as the 1964 Civil Rights Act and the 1965 Voting Rights Act, and executive actions such as Attorney General Robert Kennedy's determination to enforce desegregated interstate transportation rulings. Without the civil rights activists, the federal government would not have taken these actions, although those actions did not effect a total transformation of black American lives.

> This introduction establishes the measures designed to bring about change and indicates what the essay will argue about the extent and causes of these changes.

Supreme Court rulings against discrimination had some positive results. The Supreme Court ruled against segregated schools in 1954 and against segregated buses in Montgomery, Alabama, in 1956. The end of such humiliation enshrined in law obviously improved the lives of black Americans. Some schools, especially in urban areas such as Washington DC and in border states such as Kentucky, desegregated after the first Brown ruling. However, there was considerable white resistance, most famously at Central High School, Little Rock, Arkansas in 1957. It was 1960 before Central High was integrated and 1972 before all Little Rock schools were. The Supreme Court's lack of powers of enforcement was a frequent problem. When the Freedom Riders demonstrated that Morgan and Boynton were being ignored, it took the Attorney General's intervention to decrease segregation on interstate transport and it took the Civil Rights Act of 1964 to finally kill off Jim Crow.

> This paragraph assesses the limited extent to which black American lives were improved by Supreme Court rulings.

The 1964 Civil Rights Act gave the federal government the legal tools to combat *de jure* segregation in public places, which in combination with the 1965 Voting Rights Act revolutionised Southern black American lives. By 1970, the number of elected black officials had increased six times over and voting power and increased representation made legislators pay more attention to black Americans. This improved black morale and thereby lives. However, dire problems remained in the big city ghettos of the North and West. In ghettos such as Chicago's South Side, black Americans lived in crowded and inadequate housing. White residents in surrounding neighbourhoods such as Cicero colluded with banks and realtors to stop black Americans moving into better and more spacious accommodation with access to superior quality schools. When Congress passed the Fair Housing Act in 1968, as a gesture to the fallen King, the legislation proved ineffective in practice in the face of determined white resistance. Ghetto desperation was attested by the rise of the Black Power movement.

> This paragraph emphasises that there were dramatic improvements in the South but not in the North.

These measures, imperfect though they proved to be, all owed something to black civil rights activists. Oliver Brown and his co-litigants needed NAACP lawyers and funding to obtain the Supreme Court's Brown ruling. Of course, sympathisers on the bench and in the federal government were essential. The Truman administration had supported the NAACP over Brown, and the eight Supreme Court justices who responded to Earl Warren's demand for unanimity were clearly and unexpectedly liberal in this instance. Similarly, the desegregation of the Montgomery buses was triggered by NAACP activists Rosa Parks and E.D. Nixon, and NAACP litigation won the Browder ruling. Black advances required black activism to prod the federal government into action – each was vital to the other. The 1964 Civil Rights Act owed much to the black activism that had exposed the injustices of Jim Crow to the nation in the sit-ins (1960), the Freedom Rides (1961), the Birmingham campaign

> While previous paragraphs focus on the extent of improvement, this paragraph focuses on the main factor(s) behind the improvements.

and the March on Washington (both 1963). Without these protests, amply covered by the national media, it is unlikely that the 1964 Act would have been passed. President Kennedy admitted that the behaviour of Bull Connor's police in response to SCLC's Birmingham campaign had inspired him to promote the civil rights bill with greater enthusiasm and urgency. President Johnson was even more determined to aid black Americans. In 1964, he worked long, hard and effectively to overcome opposition from Southern Democrats in Congress. He then tried but failed for months to get Congress to fill in the gaps in the 1964 Act that allowed Southern white registrars to continue to prevent black voting, but it took SCLC activism at Selma and the publicity surrounding Bloody Sunday to get the 1965 Voting Rights Act passed.

After 1965, black activism in the form of the Black Power movement probably hampered rather than helped the black cause. The Black Power movement alienated whites and contributed greatly to Johnson's inability to get Congress to pass helpful legislation, at least until King's assassination played upon their consciences in 1968. However, Black Power gave a considerable boost to black morale, which explains the 64 per cent black approval rating for the Black Panthers. The Black Power movement contributed to the development of courses particularly relevant to black Americans in American educational institutions, and the Black Panthers in particular did some important practical work in the ghettos in the late 1960s, as with the 40 clinics they set up to give advice on economic, health and legal issues. Such things contributed to improvements in black American lives.

> This paragraph covers how activism could be both productive and counter-productive.

Overall then, the situation of black Americans improved in some ways in the years 1954–68. The federal government responded positively to the civil rights movement: Southern blacks were freed from Jim Crow, able to participate in politics and increasingly able to attend desegregated schools. However, the situation in the bleak and impoverished ghettos of the North and West remained basically unchanged. Significantly, when little was done to aid the ghettos, it was because the federal government was distracted by the Vietnam War and hampered by white objections to rising taxes and the Black Power movement, and as a result could not or would not do any more. So, while black American activism was important to such improvements as there were in the black American situation in these years, the federal government response was obviously and always the crucial factor.

> The conclusion sums up the essay's content, tying together the essay's two strands quite neatly and arguing that the federal government was more important than activism and that there were limits as to how much it would help.

This is a good essay. It covers a range of issues, demonstrating a good level of appropriate knowledge. The essay is focused on the two interconnecting issues throughout, offering arguments for and against the two underlying contentions (that activists were vital in improvements and that black American lives did improve). The conclusion reaffirms judgements offered previously and adds persuasively that the federal government was the crucial factor in the initiation and extent of improvements.

Maintaining focus

This essay is successful because it maintains a strong focus on the question throughout. You can assess whether an essay is maintaining focus by monitoring repetition of the keywords or phrases in the question. In this question, 'civil rights activists' and 'improvements' are the key topics, and the command word is 'extent'. Go through the essay and underline the keywords in one colour and treatment of the command word in another colour.

5 Obama's campaign for the presidency, 2004–09

Barack Obama's political career to 2006 and gaining the Democratic nomination for the presidency

Obama's election as senator for Illinois

Barack Obama won election to the US Senate in 2004 because:

- he had demonstrated his commitment to public service and to 'black' issues (e.g. housing discrimination) as a black community organiser in Chicago and an Illinois state senator
- polls showed voters were attracted by his 'American Dream' life story. Despite being half white, mostly raised by middle-class white grandparents and winning a scholarship to an elite private school, he emphasised the difficulties he had faced as a black American
- the national Democratic Party was very supportive because it was desperate to win the seat and to have a black Senator
- the media focused upon him and was very positive
- his inspirational keynote address at the 2004 Democratic National Convention impressed people
- his Republican opponent was black but lived in faraway Maryland.

The importance of his political career to 2006 was that

- it showed the important role that black voters and candidates played in the Democratic Party
- his election as only the third black US senator since Reconstruction suggested increased white willingness to vote for a black candidate.

The reasons for Obama's success in gaining the Democrat nomination for the presidency

Obama defeated Hillary Clinton and won the Democrat nomination for several reasons.

The opposition

New York senator and former First Lady Clinton was expected to be the nominee but she ran a flawed campaign:

- She gave the impression that she was entitled to the nomination, which alienated some Democrats.
- She emphasised her far greater political experience, but many Democrats preferred change and something new.

- She fundraised the old-fashioned way (through one-time big donors) and raised less money than Obama.
- She failed to exploit the Internet, e.g. for fundraising and contacting supporters.
- There was a great deal of in-fighting in her poorly organised campaign team.
- Suggesting Obama was un-American alienated black voters and some white liberals.
- She continued to do important work in the Senate while Obama focused on the campaign.
- Bill Clinton made errors, e.g. he claimed Obama was only doing well because he was black, which alienated black voters.

Personality and rhetorical abilities

- Obama was an inspirational orator. His speeches tapped into the American Dream ideal.
- He seemed intelligent, self-confident, highly motivated, possessed of an inner calm and more likeable than Clinton.
- He projected an appealing youth and dynamism that the older and more experienced Clinton lacked.

New election strategies

His Internet election strategies were revolutionary:

- Money was raised from tens of thousands of small donors.
- The Obama website encouraged visitors to register their interest. Once registered, they were regularly emailed and urged to contact other Obama supporters. This inspired repeated small donations, large numbers of grassroots volunteers and a great deal of voter registration.
- A database of likely voters was created.

Policies

Obama's policies were very similar to Clinton's and included:

- a speedy US exit from the Iraq war (he had long opposed the US involvement whereas Clinton had supported it initially)
- US energy independence ('green' where possible)
- more freely available health care.

Spectrum of importance

Below is a sample exam-style question and a list of general points which could be used to answer that question. Use your own knowledge and the information on the opposite page to reach a judgement about the importance of these general points to the question posed.

Write numbers on the spectrum below the list to indicate their relative importance. Having done this, write a brief justification of your placement, explaining why some of these factors are more important than others. The resulting diagram could form the basis of an essay plan.

'Barack Obama's victory in the Democrat race in 2008 owed more to Hillary Clinton than to anything he himself did.'

How far do you agree with this statement?

1 Obama's new election strategies.

2 Hillary Clinton's mistakes.

3 Obama's personality and rhetorical abilities.

4 Obama's policies.

5 Obama's political career to 2006.

6 The nature of the Democratic Party.

◄───►

Least important   Most important

Support your judgement

Below is a sample exam-style question and two basic judgements. Read the exam question and the two judgements. Support the judgement that you agree with more strongly by adding a reason that justifies the judgement.

How accurate is it to say that Barack Obama defeated Hillary Clinton in 2008 simply because he was black?

Overall, Obama's new election strategies proved crucial

_____

_____

_____

Generally, it is fair to say that more Democrats preferred Barack Obama because he was new and represented change

_____

_____

_____

Tip: whichever option you choose you will have to weigh up both sides of the argument. You could use words such as 'whereas' or 'although' in order to help the process of evaluation.

The reasons and significance for victory in November 2008 REVISED

Obama defeated Republican candidate John McCain in the presidential election of November 2008 for several reasons.

The unpopularity of Republican President George W. Bush's policies

- Many voters feared that another Republican president would continue George W. Bush's unpopular policies, especially the war in Iraq.
- Many voters blamed Republican aversion to financial regulations for the near-collapse of the financial sector in September 2008. This began with the fall of the giant Lehman Brothers bank. The next day, McCain lost his lead in the polls and never regained it. Economic issues were the main concern of 63 per cent of voters.

Obama's personality and rhetorical abilities

- Polls showed Obama's American Dream life story continued to attract voters.
- He came across as more positive than McCain, who often seemed like a grumpy old man (he was over 70). Obama's advertisements focused on policies and most people found them more positive than McCain's, which mostly attacked Obama and the Democrats.
- Obama was more appealing and impressive in the televised debates.
- When Lehman Brothers collapsed, McCain seemed to panic but Obama gave the more reassuring response.
- The selection of Alaska governor Sarah Palin as McCain's running mate frightened many voters. She came across as ill-informed, e.g. she could not name any newspaper that she read and seemed unable to answer questions on the financial crisis during the televised presidential debates. She was chosen because she appealed to the right-wing Republicans whom McCain had never enthused, e.g. he was far more concerned about the environment than most Republicans.

Finance

Obama raised far more money than McCain:

- He intelligently exploited the Internet and encouraged small donors.
- He was the first major party presidential candidate to reject the option of accepting federal funds, because that limited the amount a candidate could use out of his own campaign funds. McCain had always taken a principled stand on money buying office, so he took the federal funds, which left him far poorer and affected his advertising capacity.

New election strategies

The Obama campaign out-spent, out-advertised and out-organised McCain's and its extensive use of the Internet was revolutionary.

The significance of his victory

Many Americans viewed Obama's victory as

- historic – a black president had been elected only 43 years after the Southern black population had been guaranteed the vote
- indicative of racial equality and a new, post-racial America.

Some were negative about the significance of his victory:

- Although some whites had voted for Obama, he had relied heavily upon the minority vote and on the number of older white voters who had stayed at home because they felt McCain was insufficiently conservative and/or they feared Sarah Palin.
- Immediately after his election, white supremacist websites collapsed under the weight of traffic.
- There were several race controversies during his first year as president, e.g. the 'birther' controversy, in which right-wing extremists tried to maintain that Obama was not a 'real' American.

The response of black Americans to his victory

Despite doubts during the election campaign that Obama was 'not black enough', there was widespread black rejoicing once he was elected. However, some black intellectuals were unenthusiastic, saying

- he won because he told white Americans what they wanted to hear, namely that racism was a thing of the past
- his election was irrelevant to the predicament of the black poor.

Spot the inference

a

High-level answers avoid excessive summarising or paraphrasing of sources, and instead make inferences from the sources and analyse their value in terms of their context. Below is a source and a series of statements. Read the source and decide which of the statements:

- infer from the source [I]
- summarise the source [S]
- paraphrase the source [P]
- cannot be justified from the source [X]

Statement	I	S	P	X
1 The speaker presents himself as epitomising the American Dream				
2 The speaker acknowledges his foreign father but tries to emphasise his American credentials				
3 The speaker declares his belief in the American Dream to which even the poorest can aspire				
4 The speaker went to one of the best schools in Hawaii				
5 The speaker's rhetoric might well have been consciously modelled upon that of Martin Luther King				
6 The speaker emphasises the patriotism of his white grandparents				

SOURCE 1

From Barack Obama's keynote address to the Democratic National Convention, July 2004.

On behalf of the great state of Illinois, crossroads of a nation, Land of Lincoln, let me express my deepest gratitude for the privilege of addressing this convention.

Tonight is a particular honor for me because, let's face it, my presence on this stage is pretty unlikely. My father was a foreign student, born and raised in a small village in Kenya. He grew up herding goats, went to school in a tin-roof shack. His father – my grandfather – was a cook, a domestic servant to the British.

But my grandfather had larger dreams for his son. Through hard work and perseverance my father got a scholarship to study in a magical place, America, that shone as a beacon of freedom and opportunity to so many who had come before.

While studying here, my father met my mother. She was born in a town on the other side of the world, in Kansas. Her father worked on oil rigs and farms through most of the Depression. The day after Pearl Harbor my grandfather signed up for duty; joined Patton's army, marched across Europe. Back home, my grandmother raised a baby and went to work on a bomber assembly line. After the war, they studied on the G.I. Bill, bought a house through F.H.A., and later moved west all the way to Hawaii in search of opportunity.

And they, too, had big dreams for their daughter. A common dream, born of two continents.

My parents shared not only an improbable love, they shared an abiding faith in the possibilities of this nation. They would give me an African name, Barack, or 'blessed,' believing that in a tolerant America your name is no barrier to success. They imagined – they imagined me going to the best schools in the land, even though they weren't rich, because in a generous America you don't have to be rich to achieve your potential.

They're both passed away now. And yet, I know that on this night they look down on me with great pride.

They stand here, and I stand here today, grateful for the diversity of my heritage, aware that my parents' dreams live on in my two precious daughters. I stand here knowing that my story is part of the larger American story, that I owe a debt to all of those who came before me, and that, in no other country on earth, is my story even possible.

Exam focus

Below is a source, a question and a sample answer on the issue of Barack Obama's election to the presidency in November 2008.

Assess the value of the source for revealing why Barack Obama defeated John McCain in 2008 and white American attitudes to black Americans.. Explain your answer, using the source, the information given about its origin, and your own knowledge about the historical context.

SOURCE 1

It is traditional for the defeated candidate in a presidential election to make a "concession speech" recognising the victory of the opposing candidate. This extract is from the concession speech made by defeated Republican Senator John McCain on 5 November 2008.

Accessed at https://www.youtube.com/watch?v=bss6lTP8BJ8

The American people have spoken, and they have spoken clearly … In a contest as long and difficult as this campaign has been, [Senator Obama's] success alone commands my respect for his ability and perseverance. But that he managed to do so by inspiring the hopes of so many millions of Americans, who had once wrongly believed that they had little at stake or little influence in the election of an American president, is something I deeply admire and commend him for achieving. This is an historic election, and I recognize the special significance it has for African-Americans and for the special pride that must be theirs tonight.

I've always believed that America offers opportunities to all who have the industry and will to seize it. Senator Obama believes that, too. But we both recognize that though we have come a long way from the old injustices that once stained our nation's reputation and denied some Americans the full blessings of American citizenship, the memory of them still had the power to wound. A century ago, President Theodore Roosevelt's invitation of Booker T. Washington to visit — to dine at the White House — was taken as an outrage in many quarters. America today is a world away from the cruel and prideful bigotry of that time. There is no better evidence of this than the election of an African-American to the presidency of the United States. Let there be no reason now for any American to fail to cherish their citizenship in this, the greatest nation on Earth. Senator Obama has achieved a great thing for himself and for his country. I applaud him for it…

I urge all Americans who supported me to join me in not just congratulating him, but offering our next president our goodwill and earnest effort to find ways to come together, to find the necessary compromises, to bridge our differences and help restore our prosperity, defend our security in a dangerous world, and leave our children and grandchildren a stronger, better country than we inherited…

I am also, of course, very thankful to Governor Sarah Palin, one of the best campaigners I have ever seen and an impressive new voice in our party for reform and the principles that have always been our greatest strength … We can all look forward with great interest to her future service to Alaska, the Republican Party and our country …

I don't know what more we could have done to try to win this election. I'll leave that to others to determine. Every candidate makes mistakes, and I'm sure I made my share of them.

The source is very useful in illuminating white attitudes, quite useful in helping to explain Obama's role in his victory, but less useful in explaining the "mistakes" that McCain made.

John McCain recognises several factors important to Obama's victory. First, he rightly acknowledges that Obama was an "inspiring" candidate, although when he suggests that Obama inspired "so many millions" who felt disfranchised, he seems to be saying that it was racial minorities and particularly black Americans that he inspired and who won the election for Obama. In some ways that was true – there was an unprecedented turnout amongst black Americans, and Hispanic Americans gave Obama's strong support. His victory certainly relied heavily upon the minority vote, but any Democrat's victory would have done so. Significantly, Obama won a little more of the white vote than previous Democrat presidential candidates – 43% compared to John Kerry's 41%. Along with the black and Hispanic voters, there were many liberal white Democrats who were enthused by the prospect of America's first black president, as demonstrated by Caroline Kennedy. Second, McCain rightly recognises Obama's "perseverance" in the campaign. One wonders if Senator McCain is recognising here how Senator Obama had so focused on the campaign that he had neglected his Senatorial duties (unlike Hillary Clinton). Third, when McCain mentions Obama's "ability", he was perhaps thinking of the rhetorical ability demonstrated in the optimistic "Yes we can" speeches that aroused rapturous audience response. November 2008 was probably too early for McCain to be thinking of Obama's new electoral strategies such as the database of likely voters and the website encouraging small donors and volunteers. Overall, despite omissions, McCain usefully helps explain Obama's role in his own victory.

Not surprisingly, McCain is less useful in explaining his own contribution to his loss. Although also directed at the nation, the concession speech was made in the presence of a Republican audience and that affects the content. Sarah Palin was an important reason for McCain's loss: her ignorance of world affairs and of financial issues swayed considerable numbers of independent voters (Obama won 8% more of the independent vote the McCain). As McCain was 70 years old and had a history of health problems, his choice of running mate had been particularly important and while Palin enthused the Republican base, she worried and maybe lost some liberal Republican voters. Obviously, McCain could not in any way attribute his loss to his vice presidential pick: he had to praise her, partly because he was addressing fellow Republicans, many of whom liked her, and partly because he chose her. McCain needed a younger, more charismatic and more right-wing running mate, because of his age, his somewhat dour personality, and because his moderation on issues such as climate change antagonised hardline Republicans. However, there were other more intelligent candidates than Sarah Palin. Clearly, when McCain admits that he made mistakes, he was right. Other mistakes included his principled stand on campaign finance, which left Obama with far more money to spend on the campaign, and his panicked response to the problems following the collapse of the Lehman Brothers bank, which contrasted sharply

This introduction could be fuller, but it serves to indicate what the answer will argue.

Own knowledge is used to give a counter-argument.

Comments on overall usefulness at the start and/or end of a paragraph help ensure focus.

with Obama's calm. Along with his own mistakes, McCain was greatly handicapped by the mistakes of President George W. Bush. When McCain talks of the president needing to leave subsequent generations "a stronger, better country that we inherited", it may be that he is implicitly referring to Bush's presidency. Bush had become toxic by the time of the election, primarily because of the Iraq war, and his administration might well have been the major reason for Obama's victory. However, even though Bush was toxic, McCain was keen to make a generous and statesmanlike concession without apportioning blame, so he does not explicitly mention the terrible legacy of Bush, especially to a Republican audience. The perceived need for generosity also explains his extravagant and unrealistic praise of Palin as "one of the best campaigners I've ever seen." Overall then, the source is not useful in explaining Obama's victory, because party loyalties make it impossible for McCain to give public recognition to 2 major reasons for his defeat – Palin and Bush.

The source is surprisingly useful in revealing white American attitudes to black Americans. McCain is trying to project himself and others as without prejudice when he says "we have come a long way" in race relations. However, many in the audience to whom he made this speech booed at the mention of Obama until McCain stopped them, and the birther controversy would soon demonstrate the racism of diehard Republicans. During the campaign, Palin had suggested to an audience that Obama was "not like us", implying that he was un-American. McCain is surely unrealistic when he says America is "a world away" from the "bigotry" of the Theodore Roosevelt era. Indeed, McCain himself contradicts this in one, and possibly two, sections of the speech. First, he gives a revealing glimpse of white American attitudes when he says "many millions" of black Americans believed that they had "little at stake or little influence" in presidential elections – that suggests a feeling of alienation and helplessness, which would obviously be a result of unfavourable white attitudes. Second, when McCain talks of America offering opportunities "to all" to work hard, one wonders whether this reflects the typical Republican attitude to black Americans, whom they perceive as all too willing to live on welfare.

> The essay could be improved with more balance on the two debates – the treatment of the first debate is far longer than that of the second debate.

Overall then, the source is quite useful in explaining Obama's contribution to his victory but of little use in explaining McCain's contribution. McCain's purpose was to be gracious and statesmanlike, not to analyse the reasons for his defeat – as he says, he will leave that to others. Finally, amidst McCain's moderate and conciliatory tone are indications of unfavourable white American attitudes toward black Americans – the sort of unwitting testimony that makes a source exceptionally useful.

> The conclusion is brief, but it is a reminder that the argument has been consistent throughout the answer.

This is a good answer. The candidate is totally focused on the question and analyses the source material with suitable references to context. The candidate offers a valid, if limited, conclusion.

Reverse engineering

Read the essay and the comments and try to work out the general points of the plan used to write the essay. Once you have done this, note down the specific examples used to support each general point

You might find it worthwhile remembering this checklist when you are working on source questions such as the one above in your examination.

	FIRST DEBATE	SECOND DEBATE
Valuable		
Not valuable		
Knowledge of context used		
Brief, apposite quotations used		
Tone		
Provenance		
Purpose		

Theme 1 The changing geography of civil rights issues

The changing geographical distribution of black Americans, 1850–2009

Background

In 1850, four million of America's 23 million people were black. Most of the four million lived in the South and their mobility was restricted by their enslavement.

During the chaos of the Civil War, former slaves began migrating from the South. This was the beginning of a controversial process whereby the Southern race problem was transplanted to the rest of the United States. Most black Americans found they were not welcomed by the white population of the North and West.

Freedom in 1865

After the South's defeat and the passage of the 13th Amendment, former slaves were free to go where they chose. Many stayed in the South because

- life improved during Reconstruction, when black Southerners were given the vote and the presence of federal troops restrained white supremacism
- migration was daunting to most freed slaves, who were illiterate and unskilled
- Northern employers and unions excluded black labour.

However, the end of Reconstruction and the development of the Jim Crow laws initiated a slow drift North.

The slow drift North

The end of Reconstruction and the introduction of Jim Crow led a considerable number of black Americans to migrate North in the late nineteenth century.

- In 1879, 20,000 black Mississippian 'Exodusters' migrated from the South to Kansas.
- Southern white fears about the economic impact of the loss of black labour helped prompt the 1880 Senate committee investigation of black migration from the South. The committee blamed 'unjust and cruel' white Southerners who deprived black Americans of their rights.
- Between 1880 and 1900, black migration from the South led Chicago's black population to rise from 6,480 to 30,150 and New York City's from 65,000 to 100,000.

Black migrants found advantages and disadvantages in life outside the South:

- many had a better life in the North
- migration helped generate greater race consciousness and activism
- whites attacked the black population and colluded in various methods of race control.

Northern white methods of race control included:

- violence (as in New York City in 1900)
- gerrymandering, e.g. in 1897, Boston's City Council redrew electoral districts to dilute the impact of the black vote
- by 1891, 30 states in the North and West had adopted the secret ballot partly in order to exclude illiterate black voters
- white landowners and landlords usually refused to sell or rent homes to blacks in areas traditionally inhabited by whites
- school boards promoted *de facto* segregation
- labour unions excluded black workers.

! Complete the paragraph   a

Below is a sample question and a paragraph written in answer to this question.

The paragraph contains a point and specific examples, but lacks a concluding analytical link back to the question. Complete the paragraph, adding this link back to the question in the space provided.

> How accurate is it to say that the end of Reconstruction and the introduction of Jim Crow laws constitutes the most important turning point in the changing geographical distribution of black Americans in the years 1850–2009?

The end of Reconstruction and the introduction of the Jim Crow laws saw the start of a slow drift North in the last two decades of the nineteenth century. This was attested by population statistics: between 1880 and 1900, black migration from the South led Chicago's black population to rise from 6,480 to 30,150 and New York City's from 65,000 to 100,000. Overall,

_____

_____

_____

↕ Eliminate irrelevance   a

Below is a sample exam-style question and a paragraph written in answer to this question. Read the paragraph and identify parts of the paragraph that are not directly relevant to the question. Draw a line through the information that is irrelevant and justify your deletions in the margin.

> To what extent were economic factors the main reason for the changing geographical distribution of black Americans in the years 1850–2009?

In the late nineteenth century, economic factors were important in the migration of black Americans from the South. Migrants were hopeful that they could earn more money in the factories of cities such as Chicago and New York. Southern white fears about the economic impact of the loss of black labour helped prompt the 1880 Senate committee investigation of black migration from the South. However, there were other far more important factors, especially the desire to escape from white oppression in the South, whether in the form of slavery or in the Jim Crow laws. It is significant that during the years of congressional Reconstruction, when that oppression eased, there was little black migration.

The first Great Migration c1910–30

Around 1.6 million black Southerners migrated North from c1910–1930. They left the South because of

- Jim Crow
- the greater incidence of lynching in the South, e.g. a Georgia mob lynched 11 blacks in May 1918
- the over-dependence of parts of the South on the cotton crop. Overproduction led to frequent slumps (e.g. in 1913–15, 1920) and lower wages. Bad weather or disease could ruin the cotton crop, e.g. 500,000 black cotton workers migrated North from South Carolina after a bad harvest in 1922.

Black migrants were attracted to the North because:

- more and better jobs were available
- wages were higher, especially in the First World War, e.g. in 1918, a Northern factory worker could earn $3.25 daily, compared to $0.75 for agricultural workers down South
- when the First World War disrupted immigration from Europe, Northern employers were short of labour and actively recruited black workers
- migrants told Southern relatives and friends of more pay and less prejudice up North
- black communities in Northern cities welcomed further migrants.

Migration had disadvantages:

- Family, friends and familiar surroundings were left behind.
- Northern white racial prejudice could make it difficult to find employment.
- The cost of living was higher.
- Urban accommodation was hard to find, crowded and expensive. Northern ghettos were *de facto* segregated, overcrowded and violent, while housing and schools were poor.
- Black migrants exacerbated racial tensions and there were many race riots, especially after the First World War, when blacks were perceived as competition for jobs and housing. That led to race riots in 25 cities in 1919, e.g. Chicago.

The second Great Migration c1940–70

Around five million black Southerners migrated North and West between 1940 and 1970. During the Second World War, around two million black Americans sought well-paid employment in defence industries in Northern and West Coast cities, e.g. Oakland and Los Angeles. This migration had significant consequences.

- Increasingly dense concentrations of black populations in Northern cities led to greater black consciousness and political power; e.g. in 1941, black trade union leader A. Philip Randolph's promise to bring Washington DC to a standstill forced President Roosevelt to promote equality in the defence industries that employed two million black Americans.
- Dramatic changes in the racial composition of some cities (Chicago's black population rose from 250,000 in 1940 to 500,000 in 1950) and wartime overcrowding contributed to race riots, e.g. in Detroit, a centre of defence industries, nine whites and 25 blacks died and 800 people were injured in a 1943 riot.

Migration back to the old South

In the late twentieth century, many black Americans migrated to the South because:

- Northern ghettos continued to deteriorate
- the South changed dramatically after the 1960s
- *de facto* segregation was less pronounced in the South, e.g. Atlanta
- the South was less violent
- more black Americans held office in the South than in any other region; e.g. Houston mayor Lee Brown was a migrant
- the cost of living was lower
- while the Northern 'Rust Belt' was in decline (e.g. Detroit), companies flocked to the booming South where unions were less powerful, regulations lighter and land cheaper, and local and national government offered tax breaks
- many felt they were returning to their ancestral home; some returned to be with and/or take care of ageing relatives
- the South had a more temperate climate than the North and Midwest.

Cover the chronology

Section C questions cover a time period of at least 100 years and require you to focus on change over time. In order to do well in Section C your answer must cover the whole chronology. Therefore you will need to refer to factors, details or aspects of the entire period.

Below is a sample Section C question. Read the question and select three factors, details or aspects of the period that you can use to answer the question. Make sure one comes from the beginning of the period, one comes from the end of the period and one comes from the period in the middle.

Annotate the timeline to show where the three issues that you have selected fit. Make sure you have one in each of the three shaded areas.

> To what extent was war the most significant factor in the changing geographical distribution of black Americans in the years 1850–2009?

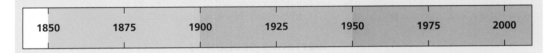

| 1850 | 1875 | 1900 | 1925 | 1950 | 1975 | 2000 |

Developing an argument a

Below is a sample exam-style question on the issue of the most important turning point in the changing geographical distribution of black Americans in our period, a list of key turning points that need to be covered in the essay and a version of a paragraph on the First World War. Read the question, the plan and the sample paragraph. Rewrite the paragraph in order to develop an argument. Your paragraph should answer the question directly and set out the evidence that supports your argument. Crucially, it should develop an argument by setting out a general answer to the question and reasons that support this.

> How far can the First World War be regarded as the key turning point in the changing geographical distribution of black Americans in the United States in the period 1850–2009?

Key points:

- The Civil War.
- The introduction of the Jim Crow laws.
- The first Great Migration.
- The second Great Migration.
- The late twentieth century return to the South.

> Around 1.6 million black Southerners migrated North between 1910 and 1930, and most of those did so during the First World War. Northern employers actively recruited black workers because the war cut off their supply of East European immigrant labour. Pay was better in the North, and black Americans already resident there told Southern friends and relations that life improved without Jim Crow and with the ability to vote.

The changing pattern of settlement and segregation 1850–2009

REVISED

Mass migration into Harlem from 1905

Harlem, New York City, illustrates the impact and significance of the changing geographical distribution of black Americans.

Reasons why mass migration into Harlem occurred after 1905

- A real estate price crash made property cheap, so landlords were desperate for tenants of any colour.
- Black real estate entrepreneur Philip Payton Jr. brought in black tenants through his Afro-American Realty Company.
- Race riots in areas of New York City previously favoured by black Americans, coupled with the demolition of some black tenements in order to make way for a railroad station, led many black New Yorkers to seek new accommodation.
- Increasing numbers of black Southerners migrated North during the first Great Migration, which began c1910 and accelerated during the First World War (1914–18) due to employment opportunities arising from the rapid, large-scale production of munitions.

Reasons why the mass migration was significant

- Between 1890 and 1920, New York City's black population rose from 70,000 to 200,000, reflecting the dramatic impact of the Great Migration on urban demography.
- Between 1920 and 1930, around 100,000 black migrants arrived in Harlem but over 100,000 whites exited, demonstrating the racial tensions that arose from the Great Migration.
- The concentration of large numbers of black Americans in an urban area generated a sense of togetherness and empowerment and helped make Harlem into a black activist and cultural centre. The Great Migration had made Harlem the unofficial black capital of the United States.

Examples of leading organisations and activists based in Harlem

- The NAACP's Harlem chapter, established in 1910, was the most influential of the nation's chapters.
- The scholar **W.E.B. Du Bois**, who founded the NAACP's *The Crisis* magazine in 1910 and edited it until he resigned in 1934.
- A. Philip Randolph, who in 1925 established the Brotherhood of Sleeping Car Porters, the first significant black labour union.
- **Marcus Garvey**, Jamaican-born leader of the United Negro Improvement Association (UNIA). Garvey moved to Harlem in 1916. His organisation attracted millions of black urbanites – far more than the NAACP. Garvey advocated black self-help, armed self-defence and the separation of the races (he emphasised 'black is beautiful').

Harlem's problems

- Poor relations between the black community and white police officers led to periodic riots, e.g. 1935, 1943.
- Poverty was a major cause of ill-health, e.g. Harlem's infant mortality rate was twice that of New York City's whites.
- Rents were high because black people were unwelcome in other parts of New York City.
- Schools were overcrowded and decaying.
- Cocaine addiction, prostitution and homicides were common.
- Most Harlemites were unskilled workers and Harlem's unemployment problems were particularly bad during the Great Depression.
- Even when there were jobs available in New York City, white racism made it difficult for black workers, e.g. in 1941, one-third of Harlemites were unemployed or on relief and in December only 142 Harlemites were working in the 30,000 war-related jobs available in New York City. That encouraged A. Philip Randolph to threaten his March on Washington and President Roosevelt to respond with the Fair Employment Practices Commission, which increased black employment opportunities in defence industries.

Harlem remained a centre of black culture and activism. Harlemites were impressed by Malcom X and the Nation of Islam in the 1950s and enthusiastic about the Black Power movement in the 1960s. Harlem frequently erupted in riots in the 1960s, but ghetto conditions were still dire in 2009. The dreams of most of the participants in the Great Migration had not been realised.

Spectrum of importance

Below is a sample exam-style question and a list of general points which could be used to answer that question. Use your own knowledge and the information on the opposite page to reach a judgement about the importance of these general points to the question posed.

Write numbers on the spectrum below the list to indicate their relative importance. Having done this, write a brief justification of your placement, explaining why some of these factors are more important than others. The resulting diagram could form the basis of an essay plan.

How far can mass migration into Harlem from 1905 be regarded as the key turning point in the changing geography of civil rights issues?

1 The organisations and individuals in Harlem.

2 The First World War.

3 Race riots.

4 The imposition of Jim Crow.

5 The Second World War.

6 The civil rights legislation of 1964-5.

Least important   Most important

Recommended reading

Below is a list of suggested further reading on this topic.

David Brown and Clive Webb, *Race in the American South* (2007)

Jonathan Gill, *Harlem* (2011)

Isabel Wilkerson, *The Warmth of Other Suns: The Epic Story of America's Great Migration* (2010)

Riots, part 1

When the Great Migration led to larger black communities in the North, racial tensions and riots increased. Soon after the First World War ended, hundreds were killed in race riots in 25 cities. The worst riots were in Chicago.

Riots in Chicago 1919

The 1919 Chicago riots were due to:

- white resentment at the increasing number of black Americans in Chicago (around 50,000 arrived between 1910 and 1920)
- white opposition to black Americans moving into white neighbourhoods
- returning white servicemen viewing blacks as competition for scarce jobs and housing
- whites resentment over increasing black political influence in local elections, e.g. Oscar De Priest became Chicago's first black alderman in 1915
- an incident on a Lake Michigan beach.

In 1919, a 15-year-old black youth accidentally strayed into the 'white' section of a segregated Chicago beach that extended into Lake Michigan. Whites stoned him, black Chicagoans protested and white police arrested them. This triggered two weeks of rioting in which:

- Irish and Polish workers, police officers and the military viciously attacked black ghetto residents
- 15 whites and 25 blacks were killed, 500 people were injured and white mobs set fire to and destroyed the homes of over 1,000 black families.

The governor of Illinois commissioned a report to explain the violence. The report recommended desegregation and blamed the riots on:

- white police mistreatment of black Americans
- ghetto living conditions
- increasing black 'race consciousness'.

Tulsa 1921

The riots in Tulsa, Oklahoma, in 1921 had similar causes to those in Chicago:

- White Oklahoman opposition to racial mixing was demonstrated when the state introduced a law making residential segregation mandatory in 1916.
- After the First World War, race relations deteriorated further as returning black veterans grew more assertive. Having fought for a country that had declared itself to be fighting for a better world, they believed that they deserved equality.
- White residents of Tulsa resented black prosperity. The Greenwood district of Tulsa, Oklahoma, contained America's wealthiest black community.
- In 1921, tensions rose amidst rumours that a black male had assaulted a white female.
- Blacks and whites armed themselves. A white mob attacked the Greenwood neighbourhood and
  - over 1,000 black houses were burned down
  - around 10,000 black Americans were left homeless
  - possibly as many as 300 black Americans died
  - up to 800 whites were injured.

Ghetto growth and riots

The Great Migration accelerated the development of *de facto* segregation and large black inner-city ghettos. Periodic race riots continued, particularly during the Second World War when troop movements and defence industries caused severe urban housing shortages that triggered dozens of race riots across America, especially in 1943, e.g. nine whites and 25 blacks died and around 800 people were injured in Detroit. America's declared opposition to fascism encouraged black Americans to become more vociferous in opposition to their own inequality.

In the decades after the Second World War, the ghettos of the North and West grew larger and more run down. America's worst ghetto riots occurred in the years 1964–68.

! Complete the paragraph   **a**

Below is a sample question and a paragraph written in answer to this question.

The paragraph contains a point and specific examples, but lacks a concluding analytical link back to the question. Complete the paragraph, adding this link back to the question in the space provided.

> To what extent did migration improve the lives of black Americans in the years 1850–2009?

Black Americans suffered during major race riots in the First Great Migration period, most famously in Chicago in 1919 and in Tulsa in 1921. Those riots had similar causes. Returning white servicemen viewed black Americans as competition for scarce jobs and housing, especially when participation in the First World War had clearly made black servicemen more assertive. Jealousy was an important factor: in Chicago, black political influence was increasing, as attested by the election of Oscar De Priest as the city's first black alderman in 1915; in Tulsa, black prosperity was evident in Greenwood. Whites believed there were certain boundaries that a black American should not cross, whether physical (the youth entering the 'white' beach on Lake Michigan triggered the Chicago riot) or sexual (the young black male who had supposedly assaulted a young white female triggered the Tulsa riots).

_____

_____

_____

ⓘ You're the examiner   **a**

Below is a sample exam-style question and a paragraph written in answer to this question. Read the paragraph and the mark scheme provided on pages 104–5. Decide which level you would award the paragraph. Write the level below, along with a justification for your choice.

> How far would you agree that race riots demonstrated failure for those who had participated in the Great Migration?

White residents of Tulsa resented black prosperity and in particular the Greenwood district, which contained America's wealthiest black community. In 1921, tensions rose amidst rumours that a black male had assaulted a white female. Blacks and whites armed themselves. A white mob attacked the Greenwood neighbourhood and over 1,000 black houses were burned down, around 10,000 black Americans were left homeless, possibly as many as 300 black Americans died and up to 800 whites were injured.

Level:

_____

Mark:

_____

Reason for choosing this level and this mark:

_____

_____

Watts, 1965, and Newark, 1967

Each summer between 1964 and 1968 saw race riots in major American cities. Some whites blamed black extremists such as Malcolm X. In July 1964, he said America would 'see a bloodbath' that summer. Harlem rioted days later. Riots in the Watts and Newark ghettos illustrate the causes of the riots.

Watts

In the 1965 riots in Watts, Los Angeles, black mobs set fire to several blocks of stores, 34 died, 100 were injured, 3,500 looters and rioters were arrested and $40 million worth of damage was done to mostly white businesses. Why?

- Ghetto residents felt the end of segregation and the guarantee of voting rights in the South was no help to them. They wanted their grievances recognised.
- King told the press that Watts was basically the revolt of an economic underclass.

Newark

The Newark, New Jersey, riots in summer 1967 demonstrated the black antagonism to what many perceived as the 'occupying forces' of the white authorities that underlay many of the ghetto riots. In Newark:

- the underlying cause of the riots was poverty and deprivation
- some whites blamed the Black Power movement (the riots broke out the day after the announcement of plans for a Black Power conference in Newark)
- the trigger was police brutality against a local cab driver
- snipers fired at white police officers
- families stole household goods from ruined stores
- black residents accused the National Guard and state troopers (called in by the city authorities and state governor) of indiscriminately shooting looters

- over 20 died and hundreds were injured
- New Jersey Governor Richard Hughes described the riots as 'plain and simple crime' but the NAACP blamed poverty and slum life
- in 1970, Newark became the first major North-Eastern city to elect a black mayor, but ghetto conditions remained dire because white flight had eroded Newark's tax base.

President Johnson commissioned the Kerner Report on the widespread rioting. The report blamed

- economic and social deprivation
- oppressive white police officers
- unsympathetic white authorities

and recommended increased expenditure on the ghettos. That was unrealistic. Whites were tired of black protests and rioting and did not want to fund ghetto improvements during the expensive Vietnam War. In many ways, Northern whites bore responsibility for ghetto riots: they had contributed to the growth of large and impoverished black urban ghettos through:

- violence and force, e.g. in 1951, several thousand working-class whites drove the sole black family out of Chicago's Cicero suburb by looting and burning
- devices such as restrictive covenants, e.g. 90 per cent of all Chicago housing after the Second World War was subject to covenants that limited sales and rentals to whites
- federal government policies, e.g. the Federal Housing Administration (FHA) rejected mortgage applications from non-whites and Jews, and the federal government was unwilling to build sufficient federal housing units for poor black Americans
- 'white flight' from the cities to the suburbs; e.g. in California, whites moved out of increasingly black Oakland into the nearby suburb of Hayward (white departures depleted a city's tax base so the ghettos grew even more rundown).

ⓘ Turning assertion into argument 　　　　　　　　　　　a

Below is a sample exam-style question and a series of assertions. Read the exam question and then add a justification to each of the assertions to turn it into an argument.

How far did the black response to white oppression and aggression change in the years 1850–2009?

In the Jim Crow years the black response was not always submissive because . . .

_____

_____

The Chicago riots of 1919 demonstrated that whites were invariably the aggressors in the outbreak of race riots in that . . .

_____

_____

The Tulsa riots demonstrated increasing black assertiveness in the face of white aggression because . . .

_____

_____

In many ways, black rioting in the 1960s showed a willingness to advertise exasperation with white domination because . . .

_____

_____

Exodus to the suburbs, segregation in Levitt estates and increasing desegregation in the old South

REVISED

The post-1945 Northern white exodus to the suburbs

In 1920, 17 per cent of Americans lived in suburbs. By 1960, it was 33 per cent – and most of these suburbanites were white. Out of the 13 million houses built between 1948 and 1958, 11 million were in the suburbs because

- the post-war housing shortage led the Federal Housing Administration (FHA) and Veterans Administration to offer low-interest mortgages
- land and new homes were cheaper
- the increased number of cars and highways facilitated commuting
- whites wanted to escape noisy, crowded cities, where taxes were higher and there were large concentrations of impoverished black Americans.

The growth of suburbia demonstrated the *de facto* segregation of housing (and therefore of schooling) outside the South.

Developments in *de facto* segregation in Levitt estates

The most famous builders in the suburbs were the Levitt brothers. They built over 10 per cent of suburban houses. Construction of the first Levittown began in Hempstead, Long Island, in New York state in 1947. This massive suburban estate was very popular with whites because the homes were well built, spacious, relatively cheap and surrounded by good facilities, e.g. swimming pools. They were also racially exclusive. Contracts stipulated that no Levittown house could be occupied by non-whites. When a black family tried to move into a Pennsylvania Levittown in 1957, whites threw stones at them. The NAACP won a legal case against this discrimination, but the black family fled in 1961. However, the 1960s saw the first sale of a Levittown house to a black family in New Jersey.

Basically, the Great Migration had revolutionised settlement patterns in the North because:

- many whites had fled to *de facto* segregated white suburbia
- black populations remained in *de facto* segregated inner-city ghettos that were characterised by poor housing, schools, employment opportunities and health, but also by increasing race consciousness.

Ghetto conditions and race consciousness were demonstrated in the great race riots of the 1960s.

Increasing desegregation in the old South post-1970

After the 1964 Civil Rights Act and the 1965 Voting Rights Act, the South changed dramatically:

- After the civil rights legislation of 1964–65, the executive and judicial branches of the federal government promoted the integration of schools. For example, in Swann v. Charlotte-Mecklenburg (1971), the Supreme Court ruled that it was time for school desegregation to be fully implemented. School desegregation in the South peaked in 1988, when 43 per cent of black schoolchildren attended schools that were more than 50 per cent white.
- Black migration to cities and white movement to the suburbs was as common in the South as in the North. That process transformed urban demography and urban politics. The frequent election of black mayors in majority-black Southern cities helped ensure that it was difficult for *de facto* segregation to be overt, e.g. Richard Arrington was mayor of Birmingham, Alabama, from 1979 to 1999.

However, the re-segregation of Southern schools began because of

- white flight
- white enrolment in private schools
- the increasing conservatism of the Supreme Court.

In New Orleans, white enrolment in city schools fell from 33 per cent to 8 per cent between 1968 and 1993, and in 1999, a Harvard study found that the South was the US region that was re-segregating at the fastest rate.

Cover the chronology

Section C questions cover a time period of at least 100 years and require you to focus on change over time. In order to do well in Section C your answer must cover the whole chronology. Therefore you will need to refer to factors, details or aspects of the entire period.

Below is a sample Section C question. Read the question and select three factors, details or aspects of the period that you can use to answer the question. Make sure one comes from the beginning of the period, one comes from the end of the period and one comes from the period in the middle.

Annotate the timeline to show where the three issues that you have selected fit. Make sure you have one in each of the three shaded areas.

'The key factor in the changing geography of civil rights issues in the years 1850–2009 was white opposition to black neighbours.'

How far do you agree?

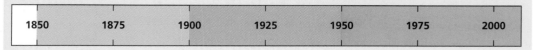

| 1850 | 1875 | 1900 | 1925 | 1950 | 1975 | 2000 |

 The flaw in the argument

Below are a sample exam-style question and a paragraph written in answer to the question. The paragraph contains an argument which attempts to answer the question. However, there is an error in the argument. Use your knowledge of this topic to identify the flaw in the argument.

How accurate is it to say that the creation of suburbs was the most significant factor in the changing geography of civil rights issues?

Black Americans congregated together in inner-city ghettos such as Chicago's South Side, while whites fled to newly constructed suburbs such as Hayward, near Oakland, in order to get away from them. The creation of suburbs deprived the cities of much of their tax base and therefore of the financial opportunity for ghetto improvements, so the creation of the suburbs was the most significant factor in the changing geography of civil rights issues, as demonstrated in the Black Power movement's focus on the ghettos.

Exam focus

Below is a sample answer to a question on the changing geography of civil rights issues in the years 1850–2009.

How far do you agree that 'push' factors were more important than 'pull' factors in black migration in the years 1850–2009?

Black migrants were motivated by a combination of 'push' and 'pull' factors. Amongst the push factors were Southern white racism and limited economic opportunities in a primarily agricultural region with excessive dependence upon a single crop. The pull factors included the promise of less racism in the North, greater employment opportunities, higher wages and the encouragement given by friends and relations already in the North. The push factors were clearly the more important, as attested by the pattern of black migration: the vast majority were willing to stay in the South during Reconstruction and growing numbers were willing to return to the South after the demise of Jim Crow in the later part of the twentieth century.

The pattern of black migration between 1865 and 1900 seems to confirm that push factors were more important than pull factors. While black mobility was obviously restricted by enslavement, slave escapees during the 1850s and the Civil War demonstrated the pre-eminence of the push factors at this time. Obviously, the desire to escape slavery was paramount. Significantly, there was no great exodus when the South offered newly freed black residents a better life after the passage of the 13th, 14th and 15th Amendments, and with the reassuring presence of federal troops to help impose Congressional Reconstruction, the vast majority of freed slaves remained in the South. It could be argued that many had little choice, given that their illiteracy and limited employable skills made migration from the South a daunting prospect. However, poor education and limited skills that would limit opportunities in the North would not stop subsequent migrants, suggesting that the push factor of the unhappy situation in the South was more important than any pull factors. When conditions deteriorated in the post-Reconstruction South, the push factors became pre-eminent again. In 1877, the federal government effectively abandoned the South, and a notable black exodus marked the transition period between Reconstruction and the establishment of Jim Crow: in 1879, 20,000 black Mississippian 'Exodusters' migrated to Kansas, which helped prompt the 1880 Senate committee investigation of black migration from the South. The committee cited the push factor of 'unjust and cruel' Southern white mistreatment as the main reason for the departure.

While Jim Crow ruled, the push factor dominated the pattern of black geographical distribution. During the first Great Migration of c1910–30, around 1.6 million black Southerners migrated North. Along with Jim Crow, there were problems with 'King Cotton'. Overproduction led to frequent slumps, as in 1913–15 and 1920, and to lower wages. Bad weather and disease frequently ruined the crop. The boll weevil was the push factor behind the migration of 500,000 black cotton workers who left South Carolina in 1922.

It is of course unwise to dismiss the strength of the pull factors, especially in war time when industry went into overdrive to produce war materiel and the major centres of defence industries were located in the North and, later, the West. In 1918, a Northern factory worker could earn $3.25 per day, while an agricultural worker in the South got around $0.75. In the Second World War, around 2 million black Americans sought well-paid employment in defence industries in cities such as Detroit, Oakland and Los Angeles. However, black living conditions and employment opportunities deteriorated dramatically after the Second World War when 'white flight' and racism promoted the growth of huge black ghettos where accommodation was low quality and expensive, schools were poor and economic opportunities limited due to

This is a good introduction, which indicates that the essay will cover various push and pull factors and will argue which was the more important.

This paragraph uses the changing pattern of migration between 1865 and 1900 to try to prove that push factors were the most important. It is particularly useful to the argument that a contemporary source opines that the push factor was crucial.

This paragraph continues with the argument that migration from the South was dictated by Southern white racism, and adds the economic weakness of the South as a push factor. The use of specific dates and statistics always strengthens an argument.

racism and to the low skill level of most ghetto residents. Black frustration with ghetto life in the North and West was demonstrated in the serial riots of 1964–68 in all major American cities, e.g., those in Watts in 1965 and Newark and Detroit in 1967. Race riots resulting from Northern white racism had been a regular feature of life outside the South ever since the Southern black population first migrated North and West. These riots surely mitigated the 'pull' attractions of the North, but clearly race relations in the South were even worse and the push factor was more important.

The black exasperation with ghetto life demonstrated in multiple ghetto riots contributed to the slow drift back to the South in the late twentieth century. Ghetto life was now the push factor, while one main pull factor was that life in the South had greatly improved since the civil rights legislation of 1964–65. First, *de facto* segregation was less pronounced in the South, in the 1970s and 1980s in particular – that was when school integration peaked. Second, more black Americans held office in the South than in any other region. Third, there were economic attractions to life in the South. The cost of living was lower and more opportunities were available now that the South's economy was more diversified. Fourth, the South had a more temperate climate than the North, which suffered brutal winters. The second great pull factor was the commonly expressed feeling that the migrants were returning to their ancestral home where many still had relations. Though presumably, had life in the North lived up to the expectations of the earlier migrants from the South, black Americans would have stayed there.

Overall, while both push and pull factors were important, the history of black migration from and back to the South suggests that the push factors of enslavement, Jim Crow and Southern economic backwardness were more significant than the pull factors of Northern and Western life, because in the periods without enslavement and Jim Crow, black Americans who came from the South often seemed to prefer to be there.

This paragraph mentions the great strength of the pull factors but tries to maintain the essay's argument by pointing out that life in the North had its problems. Ending a paragraph with a reiteration of the essay's main push argument, even though the paragraph has pointed out pull factors, might help to persuade the examiner of the argument.

This paragraph asserts that the push factor was more important in the return of some black Americans to the South, but the argument is not very persuasive.

The conclusion attempts to use the overview of the period to justify the argument that push factors were more important, but it is significant that the essay omits to mention the relatively small number of black Americans that returned to the South at the end of the twentieth century – luckily for the essay's argument, the syllabus implies that these were large numbers, although of course they were not.

This is a reasonable answer to a very difficult question. The range of push and pull factors covered demonstrates a good level of appropriate knowledge. The essay is focused on the question throughout and it tries hard to sustain its argument throughout, although it is not always persuasive.

Narrative and analytical structure

It is important that students structure an essay so that the reader is carried along by the essay's argument. Examiners dislike chronologically organised essays because they frequently lead to narrative at the expense of analysis. This essay has a chronological structure – but is it also analytical? Highlight the analysis in each of the chronological periods in this essay. When you have done that, suggest an alternative and non-chronological structure for this essay.

Theme 2 Changing portrayal of civil rights issues in fiction and film

The role of literature in shaping and reflecting changing perceptions of race relations, 1850–2009

The publication of *Uncle Tom's Cabin* (1852)

Abolitionist **Harriet Beecher Stowe**'s *Uncle Tom's Cabin* tells how the deeply religious slave Tom is sold and separated from his family. His religiosity leads to friendship with Eva, daughter of his new master, but a subsequent master kills him because of that religiosity.

Contemporary evidence recorded *Uncle Tom's Cabin*'s influence:

- A record 300,000 copies were sold in its first year.
- In 1855, a contemporary described it as the most popular current novel.
- President Lincoln supposedly greeted Stowe as the author of the book that started the Civil War (i.e. it aroused Northern anti-slavery emotions and Southern white paranoia about abolitionism).
- Southerners responded with over 20 pro-slavery novels, e.g. *Aunt Phillis's Cabin*.

Initially, leading black abolitionist Frederick Douglass praised the book, but by 1865 criticised the 'delusion' that black Americans would let themselves be whipped as Tom had. Greater black assertiveness in the twentieth century led the words 'Uncle Tom' to signify excessive deference to whites.

Illustrations and plays

The original illustrations emphasised Tom's youth, Christianity and close relationship with Eva, but illustrations in later editions made Tom elderly and dependent upon Eva's guidance in his Bible reading. That reflected changing white perceptions: slaves were helpless, freed black males were potentially threatening. *Uncle Tom's Cabin* plays followed a similar pattern. They increasingly demeaned black people, reflecting increased Northern white unease over black migration.

Overall, the character of Uncle Tom originally shaped public opinion but subsequently reflected changing white opinion after emancipation.

Adventures of Huckleberry Finn (1885)

Mark Twain's novel, written after abolition, tells how Huck escapes his evil pa and befriends runaway slave Jim. Villainous whites capture and sell Jim but Huck and his friend Tom free Jim. Jim sacrifices freedom to help Tom, who eventually reveals that Jim's former owner had freed him.

Twain's wife came from an abolitionist family and his novel was anti-slavery (Huck rejects the slaveholding 'civilisation'). However, Twain noted that the most popular section of the book was the one where the boys prolong Jim's slavery and suffering, which suggests the novel's immediate and great popularity was not due to any sympathy for Jim. No doubt Twain was seeking to engage his readers with some knockabout entertainment, but he also sometimes portrays Jim as unintelligent and dependent upon Huck – a condescending attitude that probably reflected contemporary white opinion.

Subsequently, changing attitudes affected views of *Adventures of Huckleberry Finn*. It became a standard school text and in 1957, the NAACP criticised its 'belittling racial designations'. In 1998, federal judges ruled that literature probably reflected and perhaps shaped ideas at the time of writing but later readers would recognise that it was the product of particular beliefs at a particular time, so studying the book at school would not psychologically damage black children.

! Delete as applicable

Below are a sample exam-style question and a paragraph written in answer to this question. Read the paragraph and decide which of the possible options (in bold) is most appropriate. Delete the least appropriate options and complete the paragraph by justifying your selection.

'*Uncle Tom's Cabin* reflected rather than shaped public opinion.' How far do you agree with this statement?

When the novel *Uncle Tom's Cabin* was published in 1852, it shaped rather than reflected Northern public opinion. Abolitionists in the North were only a minority, but as Harriet Beecher Stowe proved, they could be **quite influential/influential/very influential**. The extent of the book's influence was perhaps best attested by the Southerners who felt the need to write over 20 pro-slavery novels in response. However, the many plays based upon the novel and performed up until the early twentieth century were often very different from Harriet Beecher Stowe's novel. Some were even pro-slavery, and this was surely a reflection of **a little change/a fair amount of change/a great change** in the attitudes on the part of Northern white Americans to the freed slaves, because

_____

_____

! Turning assertion into argument

Below is a sample exam-style question and two assertions. Read the exam question and then add a justification to each assertion to turn it into an argument.

How far did *Adventures of Huckleberry Finn* shape and reflect perceptions of race relations in the years 1885–2009?

Views on *Adventures of Huckleberry Finn* changed in the years 1885–2009 because . . .

_____

_____

Uncle Tom's Cabin and *Adventures of Huckleberry Finn* did not have a comparable impact on white attitudes in the years 1850–2009 because . . .

_____

_____

Gone with the Wind (1936)

Atlantan Margaret Mitchell's novel told of beautiful, wilful Southern belle Scarlett O'Hara, whose family plantation Tara is devastated by the Civil War. Scarlett marries Frank Kennedy, who has the money to save Tara. Kennedy dies in a Ku Klux Klan defence of Scarlett's honour after she was attacked by a black man when driving through **shantytown**. Always fascinated by roguish Rhett Butler, she marries him, but their marriage fails. As he leaves her she says, 'Tomorrow is another day'.

The novel was a phenomenal success, topping the US fiction bestseller list in 1936–37.

Criticisms connected with race

Gone with the Wind was criticised by a few white liberals and many black Americans:

- The book uses the language of the Civil War and Reconstruction period, but 'darky' and 'nigger' were becoming less acceptable by the 1930s. Mitchell's animal imagery also created some unease, e.g. Scarlett's Mammy's face is compared to that of a monkey.

- The Tara slaves are well treated and some contemporaries criticised the loyal house slaves who remain at Tara after abolition as stereotypical, e.g. dim-witted Prissy and totally devoted Mammy.

- Mitchell was accused of romanticising the Klan, although Rhett and Scarlett's brother-in-law are quite critical of it.

- Mitchell's depiction of Reconstruction had freed slaves as unable to care for themselves as well as slave owners had done, and a black freedman's attack on Scarlett is in the tradition of wildly exaggerated Southern white fears of black freedmen as potential rapists.

Book and movie

Gone with the Wind reflected Mitchell's traditional Southern viewpoint on slavery and Reconstruction, and during the making of David Selznick's film of the novel, it was clear that liberals and black Americans feared that the popularity of both book and movie might shape views of black Americans and their history. Much of Selznick's correspondence focused on race and it suggests perceptions were changing in the 1930s. Selznick responded to the many black and white requests to excise the word 'nigger' from the film and made Scarlett's would-be rapist white, but there were still black demonstrations against the movie in several cities. In that *Gone with the Wind* promoted discussion of race, it probably helped shape a greater degree of racial sensitivity.

Both film and book remained popular – in a 2014 poll, the book emerged as the second favourite of American readers. That did not necessarily mean that it reflected and/or shaped views on race, because for many, the old South was just the necessary background against which an exploration of love and loss was set.

Develop the detail

Below is a sample exam-style question and a paragraph written in answer to this question. The paragraph contains a limited amount of detail. Annotate the paragraph to add additional detail to the answer.

'*Gone with the Wind* reflected contemporary perceptions of race.'

How far do you agree with this statement about the reception given to *Gone with the Wind* in the 1930s?

> Margaret Mitchell was born in Atlanta. Some white liberals and black Americans disliked the language she used in her novel, because they feared that it reflected and might shape racism. In the same way, they disliked her idealised view of slavery and unflattering view of freedmen.

You're the examiner

a

Below is a sample exam-style question and a paragraph written in answer to this question. Read the paragraph and the mark scheme provided on pages 104–5. Decide which level you would award the paragraph. Write the level below, along with a justification for your choice.

How accurate is it to say that *Gone with the Wind* shaped and reflected perceptions of race relations in the years 1936–2009?

> *Gone with the Wind* was a phenomenal success on first publication and has remained high on the list of American readers' favourite books ever since (it ranked second in 2014). Some white liberal and black American contemporaries regretted its treatment of race: it used language such as 'niggers', had stereotypical black characters, and its sympathies obviously lay with Margaret Mitchell's South. Those critics felt it reflected contemporary perceptions of race and obviously feared that it would shape perceptions in a negative fashion. However, the correspondence of the movie version's producer David Selznick suggested that it reflected positive change in perceptions, in that contemporary anxieties about the language and content was such that Selznick excised 'nigger' and made Scarlett's Reconstruction—era attacker a white man.

Level:

_____

Mark:

_____

Reason for choosing this level and this mark:

_____

_____

To Kill a Mockingbird (1960)

Harper Lee's novel was critically acclaimed by contemporaries and became a standard text in the American school curriculum. It tells of Alabama lawyer Atticus Finch, his son Jem and his daughter Scout. Atticus agrees to defend black American Tom Robinson against the charge of raping white trash Mayella Ewell. The townspeople criticise Atticus as a 'nigger lover'. The children save Tom from a lynching, but although Atticus discredits Mayella's testimony, the all-white jury finds Tom guilty. He is shot trying to escape.

Although set in the 1930s, the novel reflects the growing preoccupation with race at the time Lee wrote. Criticisms of the book often reflected contemporary preoccupations. In the 1960s, Southern whites criticised Mayella's attraction to a black man. In the 1970s, liberals criticised Lee for stereotyping and marginalising black characters. The late twentieth century saw some ahistorical white liberal and black criticisms, e.g. Tom needing a white man to defend him was realistic not patronising – a black lawyer was unlikely in a small Alabama town in the 1930s. Similarly, the word 'nigger' was in common usage at the times the book was set and written.

However, the vast majority of readers say the book shaped their views on race in a positive fashion – Connecticut-born teacher Wally Lamb considered its impact on the high school students he had taught for 25 years comparable to the contemporary impact of Uncle Tom's Cabin.

Beloved (1987)

Toni Morrison's novel focuses on the black community's struggle with the memory and crippling legacy of slavery. Most contemporary critics praised the book, which sold well and became a standard college text. It tells of devoted mother Sethe, who kills her daughter rather than see her enslaved. During Reconstruction, the malevolent spirit of the murdered daughter haunts the house and damages her siblings. A girl who might be the dead daughter comes to the house and leeches the life out of Sethe until the black community exorcises her.

Interestingly, the movie of Beloved was admired by critics but a box office disaster, perhaps suggesting that thoughtful books had a more receptive audience than thoughtful movies and raising the question whether complex books reflected and/or shaped the opinions of anyone other than a literate, liberal elite.

The Help (2009)

White Mississippian Kathryn Stockett's bestselling novel tells of young white college graduate Skeeter, whose liberal views on race relations differ greatly from those of other whites in Jackson, Mississippi, in the 1960s. Skeeter collates the stories of local black domestics who nurture young white children then watch them grow up to be segregationist. Their stories are widely read and Skeeter has to leave Mississippi. The domestics suffer no retribution because Jackson's leading racist does not want it known that she is the greedy employer who has eaten chocolate pie containing her sacked maid's excrement. Just about everyone who is black or liberal lives happily ever after.

The book and its movie version were very successful, perhaps because white America wanted to hear that there were good white Southerners during Jim Crow, and that exploited black domestics lived happily ever after. However, the Association of Black Women Historians derided both book and film for stereotyping and trivialising black domestic workers. They felt literature reflected and could shape perceptions of race.

ⓘ Establish criteria ◀ a

Below is a sample exam-style question which requires you to make a judgement. The key term in the question has been underlined. Defining the meaning of the key term can help you establish criteria that you can use to make a judgement.

Read the question, define the key term and then set out two or three criteria based on the key term, which you can use to reach and justify a judgement.

How far has the portrayal of the lives of black Americans in <u>fiction reflected the perceptions of black Americans</u> by the white majority in the period 1850–2009?

Definition

_____

_____

Criteria to judge the extent to which the depiction of black lives reflected white perceptions of those lives.

_____

_____

_____

_____

ⓘ Reach a judgement

Having defined the key term and established a series of criteria, you should now make a judgement. Consider how far the lives of black Americans in fiction reflected white perceptions according to each criterion. Summarise your judgements below:

Criterion 1:

_____

Criterion 2:

_____

Criterion 3:

_____

Criterion 4:

_____

Finally, sum up your judgement. Based on the criteria, how accurate is it to say that fiction reflected white perceptions of black Americans?

_____

_____

Tip: remember you should weigh up evidence of black and white approval of portrayals against black and white criticisms of portrayals in your conclusion.

The role of visual portrayals in influencing and reflecting changing perceptions of race, 1850–2009

Images of black Americans in paintings, photographs and lithographs 1850–80

1850s

In the 1850s, there were several categories of visual representations of black Americans:

- Demeaning portrayals were common, e.g. in *Harper's Weekly*, the most popular contemporary periodical, and in advertisements for the popular minstrel shows that incorporated white people in blackface. These recurrent representations portrayed black Americans as unintelligent, idle, superstitious and carefree, and surely reflected the views of many whites. White Southerners disliked the minstrel shows for their frequently sympathetic attitude toward runaway slaves, while abolitionists disliked their depiction of happy slaves.

- Abolitionist portrayals were designed to evoke sympathy for pathetic black slaves and, like Uncle Tom, they probably did.

- Black Americans commissioned pictures and photographs designed to demonstrate the similarities between black and white lives, e.g. the photograph in which black abolitionist Sojourner Truth is dressed in middle-class style.

Civil War (1861–65)

Photography was a new medium in the Civil War. Photographs of black soldiers in Union uniforms were common, symbolising a black empowerment that fascinated both photographers and those who bought the photographs.

Post-war portrayals

Post-war visual portrayals were mostly demeaning, e.g. political posters, lithograph advertisements and illustrations for *Uncle Tom's Cabin*. The 1852 Uncle Tom of Harriet Beecher Stowe's novel and of Hammatt Billings' illustrations was young, virile and able to read the Bible on equal terms with Eva. Subsequent illustrations increasingly disempowered him: he was aged and made dependent upon Eva's tuition, an unthreatening reflection of increasing white racial antagonism toward younger black males.

Birth of a Nation (1915)

In the early twentieth century, movies were a new and very popular form of entertainment and roughly half the American population went to see them. The most famous and influential of silent movies was *Birth of a Nation*, based on North Carolinian Thomas Dixon's novel *The Clansman* (1905), a pro-Ku Klux Klan novel, written in horrified reaction to the portrayal of the South in an Uncle Tom play. The movie was directed by D.W. Griffith, son of a Confederate veteran.

The film's hero is Confederate veteran Ben Cameron. The villains are lazy and stupid black Republican legislators, armed black men who try to stop white men voting, and a black soldier who tries to rape Cameron's sister. That inspires Cameron to establish the Ku Klux Klan, who lynch the black soldier and restore white control while Jesus Christ looks down in approbation.

Contemporary reactions

- *Birth of a Nation* was a phenomenal success amongst white audiences. In New York City alone, one million moviegoers saw it in its first year, despite the black riots that temporarily halted screenings in several cities. President Woodrow Wilson, a Southerner, praised it.

- Thomas Dixon claimed that it made viewers eternally pro-South.

- Catholic priest and Professor of Dramatics Father Daniel Lord recalled finding it overwhelming and concluding that this was a medium that could change attitudes to life, civilisation and customs.

- Black commentators agreed that it influenced white perceptions and behaviour. It inspired the re-establishment of the Ku Klux Klan and the NAACP blamed it for an upsurge in lynching.

! Complete the paragraph a

Below is a sample exam-style question and a paragraph written in answer to this question.

The paragraph contains a point and specific examples, but lacks a concluding analytical link back to the question. Complete the paragraph by adding this link back to the question in the space provided.

How far did the portrayal of the lives of black Americans in visual images produce a change in the perceptions of black Americans by the white majority in the period 1850–1880?

> *Demeaning portrayals were common. For example, Harper's Weekly was the most popular contemporary periodical, and its illustrations of black Americans were frequently demeaning. Similarly, minstrel shows were very popular, and advertisements for them exaggerated black features and indicated a lack of intelligence. White Southerners disliked the minstrel shows for their frequently sympathetic attitude toward runaway slaves, while abolitionists disliked their depiction of happy slaves.*
>
> _____
>
> _____
>
> _____

⬍ Develop the detail

Below is a sample exam-style question and a paragraph written in answer to this question. The paragraph contains a limited amount of detail. Annotate the paragraph to add additional detail to the answer.

How far have portrayals of black American lives in film changed white perceptions of black American lives?

> *Birth of a Nation was a phenomenal box office success. There were both black and white Americans who felt that the portrayal of black American lives had changed white perceptions. Thomas Dixon claimed that audiences went away pro–South and Father Daniel Lord recalled finding it overwhelming. The NAACP and black commentators criticised it.*

In the Heat of the Night (1967)

By the 1960s, movies were beginning to challenge racial stereotypes and attitudes. Hollywood responded to NAACP insistence upon more black characters, and **Sidney Poitier** became a top star. Most of his 1960s' film roles were blandly integrationist, unthreatening and acceptable to moderate whites.

The movie *In the Heat of the Night* was based on John Ball's novel. In the 1960 novel, the black hero was not an angry young man, but by 1967, when the movie was made, America had experienced the civil rights movement, the end of Jim Crow and the Black Power movement. The movie sharpened the racial antagonisms, thereby reflecting the contemporary context.

In this movie, black Philadelphia detective Virgil Tibbs (Sidney Poitier) passes through a Mississippi town. He is arrested as a murder suspect, simply because he is black. When local white police chief Bill Gillespie discovers Tibbs is a detective, they work together and solve the murder. Gillespie grows to respect Tibbs.

Significance

The movie is considered a telling reflection of contemporary racial attitudes:

- In the book, Tibbs does nothing when a racist he is questioning slaps him. In the movie, Tibbs slaps him back. This perhaps reflects Hollywood's growing acceptance of black assertiveness.

- Sidney Poitier maintained that he had insisted on the return slap, but the white director and the screenwriter said this had always been in the script. This perhaps reflects Sidney Poitier's unease at black criticisms of him for portraying sanitised black characters.

- Hollywood always worried about offending Southern white audiences, but the film was made cheaply so it could afford their absence. The cast and crew met considerable white antagonism on location down South. This reflected that diehard racism remained quite common amongst Southern whites.

- The movie was one of the most popular pictures of 1967. It could be argued that this reflects increasing acceptance of liberal views on the part of whites, or that there were other factors: it was a good and atmospheric tale, many people like to see Academy Award winners and many liked to see Sidney Poitier.

- At the Academy Awards, Academy President Gregory Peck said, 'Society has always been reflected in its art, and one measure of Dr King's influence on the society in which we live is that of the five films nominated for Best Picture of the Year, two deal with the subject of understanding between the races' (the second was another Poitier vehicle, the interracial romance *Guess Who's Coming to Dinner*). Perhaps Peck was right; perhaps the civil rights movement had made white Americans (or at the very least liberals in Hollywood) more sympathetic to black Americans and to what they had suffered in the South.

- Most critics were positive and some particularly liked it when the Tibbs character had to learn racial tolerance too, but a minority disagreed. Critic Andrew Sarris, writing at a time when opposition to school desegregation continued, thought it a 'fantasy of racial reconciliation'.

Overall, the film perhaps reflected a change in attitude in that more whites hoped for greater racial tolerance. However, it is difficult to argue that the film had any positive influence: it was at this time that President Lyndon Johnson was trying and failing to get Congress to pass more civil rights legislation.

! Mind map

Use the information on the page opposite to add detail to the mind map below to show the causes of the exclusion of black voters.

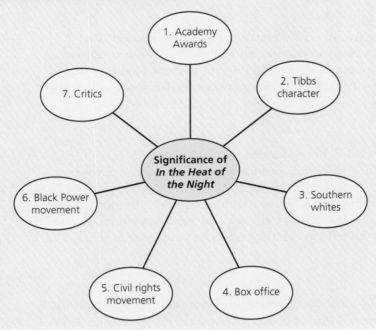

⬍ Support your judgement

Below is a sample exam-style question and two basic judgements. Read the exam question and the two judgements. Support the judgement that you agree with more strongly by adding a reason that justifies the judgement.

How accurate is it to say that white audiences disliked assertive black characters in movies in the years 1850–2009?

Overall, *In the Heat of the Night* was simply a fantasy of racial reconciliation and had no real contemporary relevance

_____

_____

_____

Generally, *In the Heat of the Night* reflected changing white perceptions of black Americans

_____

_____

_____

Tip: whichever option you choose you will have to weigh up both sides of the argument. You could use words such as 'whereas' or 'although' in order to help the process of evaluation.

More black actors

1950s

During the 1950s, television became America's most popular form of entertainment. The NAACP claimed that although black entertainers were commonly seen on TV, black characters in drama series were stereotypes, e.g. devoted servants. In 1967, the Kerner Commission had recommended that more black actors should be used and this recommendation was increasingly followed by both blacks and whites.

1969–74

Between 1969 and 1974, independent black filmmakers made 'blaxploitation' films, with action-packed adventures in the ghettos. These reflected contemporary black radicalism and were criticised by some middle-class black Americans and by the NAACP, who felt they glorified violence, drug dealing, gangsters and black studs. White audiences, especially the young, went to see these films, reflecting white willingness to accept all-black casts – and movie demonisation of whites. It is difficult to tell whether this reflected white sympathy, or just a desire to see a fashionable action movie.

1970s

In the 1970s, the TV station CBS ran 'social consciousness' programmes such as the popular *All in the Family* (1971–79). The liberal writers of that series were surprised and disappointed to find that many people agreed with the sentiments expressed by their central character, white bigot Archie Bunker. In this contemporary context, the ABC drama series *Roots* was revolutionary.

Roots was Alex Haley's fictionalised account of the enslavement of his ancestors. Kunta Kinte, a black warrior in West Africa, is captured and sold into slavery in Maryland. He and his descendants meet many unpleasant whites – slave traders, slaveowners, an overseer who likes the whip, slave catchers who chop off Kunta Kinte's foot, white rapists, Klansmen and a senator who exploits sharecroppers. The black characters are the 'good guys' and white characters are mostly 'bad guys'. In the end, Kunta Kinte's descendants are free and farm their own land.

ABC feared that white audiences would not like their series, but a record-breaking 100 million watched the last episode – half the American population. It is possible that whites liked the series because their attitude to the black American past had changed or because:

- The cast was top quality. It included many familiar white actors and it inserted in the story a character who would make whites feel better about their race – a slave captain with a conscience.

- It was an American Dream story focused upon family life, to which whites could easily relate.

Critics loved *Roots* and it accustomed white viewers to watching predominantly black actors. It is possible that it had a positive impact on some white attitudes, but there is no hard evidence that it did so. Racial antagonism remained a key feature, as seen in the continuing contemporary opposition to integrated schools, and the ghettos remained without help, as would be seen in the television drama series *The Wire* (2002–08).

Support or challenge? ⓐ

Below is a sample exam-style question which asks you to what extent you agree with a specific statement. Below that is a list of general statements which are relevant to the question. Using your own knowledge and the information on the opposite page, decide whether these statements support or challenge the statement in question.

How far do you agree that *Roots* had a positive impact upon white perceptions of black American lives?

STATEMENT	SUPPORT	ARGUABLE	CHALLENGE
100 million Americans watched the last episode.			
Critics praised it.			
In 1977, the ghettos remained impoverished, with poor quality schools, overcrowded and decaying housing and high crime rates.			
The black characters in *Roots* were invariably 'good guys'.			

The flaw in the argument ⓐ

Below are a sample exam-style question and a paragraph written in answer to the question. The paragraph contains an argument which attempts to answer the question. However, there is an error in the argument. Use your knowledge of this topic to identify the flaw in the argument.

To what extent was *Roots* a turning point in white perceptions of black American lives in the years 1850–2009?

The significance of *Roots* lay in that it was one of the first amongst movies or TV series to have a predominantly black cast and to be very popular with white audiences. A white-dominated TV channel showed the drama series, nearly half the US population watched the final episode and critics praised it, all of which indicates that *Roots* marked a turning point in white perceptions of black American lives.

Mississippi Burning (1988)

Hollywood rarely explored the dramatic struggles of the civil rights movement. One of the few examples was *Mississippi Burning*, which told of the FBI investigation into the murder of three civil rights activists during the Mississippi Freedom Summer of 1964. The film focuses upon two white FBI agents who find the murderers in the face of uncooperative Southern law enforcement officials and townspeople.

Many critics were positive, although black activists and the influential *Washington Post* questioned why such a movie focused upon white FBI agents rather than upon black activists. One black critic resented the portrayal of black Americans as passive in the face of violence, at a time of brave civil rights activism.

Perhaps such conflicting reactions help explain why Hollywood mostly avoided the subject. Another explanation could be that the film was not a massive hit. Perhaps white audiences were tired of black victims of white racism. Significantly, white audiences liked the all-black *Boys 'n' the Hood* (1991), which explored the problems of black youth without blaming white racism.

Malcolm X (1992)

A series of controversies over the movie confirmed that films about black Americans could be minefields:

- The first-choice director was white, which angered some black Americans including Spike Lee.
- Some black nationalists opposed the choice of Spike Lee as director because they thought his Malcolm would be distorted to appeal to the black middle class.
- An article in the *American Historical Review* (1994) criticised the movie for glossing over the 'weirder' Nation of Islam beliefs, and said the emphasis on Malcolm's clash with the cops reflected 1990s tensions rather than Malcolm's experiences.
- Critics loved the film but it was only a moderate box office success – black Americans constituted the majority of the audiences, so the movie had little or no opportunity to influence white America. The composition of the audiences probably reflected white ambivalence about Malcolm.

The Wire

White Baltimore journalist David Simon set this TV drama in the decayed industrial seaport of Baltimore. It ran for five seasons on the prestigious cable channel HBO. Each season had a different focus:

1 Drug trade in the decaying **projects**.
2 Predominantly white labour unions struggling with the port's decline.
3 Predominantly black and corrupt city government.
4 Crumbling school system failing ghetto children.
5 Declining white-dominated newspaper industry.

Both black and white characters were flawed, in varying degrees. Most crimes were committed by black Americans, but Baltimore is a majority-black city and the drama portrayed them as trapped in ghettos and crime with few opportunities to escape.

Most critics thought *The Wire* was about class not race. It contains very little racial tension (the virtual absence of white police brutality against black Americans was unrealistic), which along with a prominent black and white romance might reflect a post-racial society or more likely Simon's hopes for one. Another way in which *The Wire* might be considered to reflect the white liberal racial viewpoint was the low audiences: season 4 averaged only 1.6 million viewers per episode. As with *Beloved*, it seems mass white audiences were not keen on being educated on black problems – unless, like Kunta Kinte's descendants, they had a happy ending. When Simon said, 'Fuck the average viewer', he was suggesting that, in this case, the media reflects and influences attitudes to a very limited extent.

Section C questions cover a time period of at least 100 years and require you to focus on change over time. In order to do well in Section C your answer must cover the whole chronology. Therefore you will need to refer to factors, details or aspects of the entire period.

Below is a sample Section C question. Read the question and select three factors, details or aspects of the period that you can use to answer the question. Make sure one comes from the beginning of the period, one comes from the end of the period and one comes from the period in the middle.

Annotate the timeline to show where the three issues that you have selected fit. Make sure you have one in each of the three shaded areas.

How far has the portrayal of black American lives in fiction and film changed white perceptions of black Americans in the period 1850–2009?

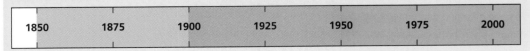

| 1850 | 1875 | 1900 | 1925 | 1950 | 1975 | 2000 |

Below is a list of suggested further reading on this topic.

Donald Bogle, *Toms, Coons, Mulattos, Mammies, & Bucks* [2001].

Mark Harris, *Pictures at a Revolution: Five Movies and the Birth of a New Hollywood* [2008].

Mary McDonagh Murphy, *Scout, Atticus and Boo: A Celebration of To Kill a Mockingbird* [2010].

Mary Ann Watson, *Defining Visions: Television and the American Experience in the Twentieth Century* [2008].

Exam focus

Below is a sample question and a sample answer on the issue of the changing portrayal of civil rights issues in fiction.

How far has the portrayal of race relations in fiction produced a change in the perceptions of black Americans by the white majority in the years 1850–2009?

Throughout the period 1850–2009 there have been commentators who considered that fiction had the capacity to influence and change perceptions, ranging from Abraham Lincoln who in the mid-nineteenth century supposedly thought the character of Uncle Tom helped provoke Northern white sympathy and the Civil War, to the Association of Black Women Historians who in the early twenty-first century thought *The Help* would give readers the wrong perception of black American domestics in the early 1960s. However, there are perhaps only two novels that might be considered to have changed white perceptions. These are *Uncle Tom's Cabin* and *To Kill a Mockingbird*. For the most part, fiction usually reflected rather than changed white opinion.

This is a reasonably focused introduction that says what the essay will argue.

Lincoln had a point when he supposedly blamed *Uncle Tom's Cabin* for the Civil War. The book sold phenomenally well. Readers' sympathy for Uncle Tom helped arouse Northern anti-slavery emotions, so much so that Southerners responded with over 20 pro-slavery novels, such as *Aunt Phillis's Cabin*. In 1988, the historian James McPherson opined that the reason for the novel's impact was that it was the story of the break-up of the family, and readers could respond to that. However, while the book might well have changed Northern white perceptions of slavery, it did not generate any long-lasting sympathy for black Americans. This was clearly demonstrated when late-nineteenth-century black migrants experienced racism and riots in the North. White opinion was indeed changing, but not necessarily for the better. The change was reflected in the illustrations of later editions of *Uncle Tom's Cabin* and in the Uncle Tom plays: some of the plays were pro-slavery, and many of them portrayed black Americans unfavourably. Hammatt Billings' illustrations for the first edition of *Uncle Tom's Cabin* showed Tom as Harriet Beecher Stowe described him – young, virile and able to read the Bible on equal terms with Eva. However, in later editions he was elderly and needed Eva's help to read. Changing white perceptions of black males (once freed they were perceived as threatening) shaped the subsequent portrayals, suggesting that although the original Uncle Tom probably helped turn many whites against the institution of slavery, he had not managed to change white people's perception of black people (as opposed to simply enslavement) for the better.

This paragraph attempts to evaluate whether *Uncle Tom's Cabin* changed white perceptions and argues 'yes' over slavery but 'no' over black Americans in general – an interesting distinction.

Perhaps it has only been *To Kill a Mockingbird* (1960) that really changed white perceptions of black Americans and race relations. The book became a standard in the American school curriculum and many readers attested that it had shaped their views on race in a positive fashion. For example, Connecticut-born teacher and novelist Wally Lamb considered its impact on the high school students he had taught for 25 years comparable to the contemporary impact of *Uncle Tom's Cabin*.

This paragraph, like the last one, continues to explore the argument set out in the introduction and offers testimonies that a book has changed attitudes.

It is difficult to see other notable fictional portrayals doing anything other than confirming white perceptions. Mark Twain's *Adventures of Huckleberry Finn* seems to illustrate the contemporary ambivalence toward black Americans, although of course it is important to differentiate the views of the author from those of his creation. The prolongation of Jim's slavery and anguish through the actions of Huckleberry Finn and Tom Sawyer seems to reflect an unnecessarily cruel and heartless attitude – and it is significant that this section of the novel, with its knockabout comedy, was noted by Mark Twain as being the most popular part of the book. Clearly, *Adventures of Huckleberry Finn* did not produce any positive change in white perceptions, but rather confirmed white lack of concern for black Americans – if not by Mark Twain, who was almost certainly aiming to make his book more interesting, then on the part of his readers.

In *Adventures of Huckleberry Finn*, Jim was often portrayed as unintelligent and childishly dependent upon the young Huckleberry, and there were similar depictions in Margaret Mitchell's *Gone with the Wind* (1936). Some white liberals and some black Americans disliked the language of Mitchell's book ('darky' and 'nigger') and the portrayal of the black characters such as dim and hysterical Prissy and ultra-loyal Mammy. There is no doubt that Atlanta-born Mitchell, who had listened to her grandmother's stories of the wonderful life in the ante-bellum South and of the awfulness of the Reconstruction, had a typical Southern white view of black Americans and their role in Southern history. Her perception of black Americans was probably shared by most white Americans, one notable exception being the producer of the movie version of the book. Producer David Selznick changed the colour of the would-be rapist in the shantytown and excised some offensive words. *Gone with the Wind* could conceivably have changed some people's views for the worse because of its pro-Southern white sympathies, but it might also have changed some views for the better in that it seems to have provoked heated and productive debate about its treatment of the black characters. The debate can be seen in Selznick's correspondence during the making of the movie and it suggests that Mitchell's great novel might have mobilised white liberals and black Americans to draw attention to how fictional portrayals could be highly offensive to some people. However, given that it was the 1930s, before Southern black Americans were liberated from Jim Crow, it seems safe to assume that *Gone with the Wind* did not change white perceptions in a positive way.

After the liberation of black Americans from Jim Crow, fictional depictions of black Americans frequently served to stimulate debate about race relations. This can be seen in the two most recent bestsellers dealing with the topic, *Beloved* (1987) and *The Help* (2009). Like *To Kill a Mockingbird*, *Beloved* quickly became a standard text, although for college students rather than for schoolchildren. As college students were generally considered to be something of an intellectual elite, one would imagine that they were already aware of the connection between black history and current black problems. Given that, it is hard to imagine that the book changed white perceptions of black Americans.

The Help was a far more comforting version of black history, in which black domestics in the 1960s were assisted in their progression from drudgery and lack of appreciation to authors who shared royalties – and all thanks to a white liberal. *The Help* reflected rather than shaped white attitudes – it no doubt suited white audiences to think that there had been whites who had stood up against segregation in Mississippi in the early 1960s, just as it suited many whites to believe that the election of Barack Obama signalled the advent of a post-racial society.

Overall then, fiction has mostly served to reflect contemporary white attitudes to black Americans and perhaps *Uncle Tom's Cabin* and *To Kill a Mockingbird* are the only novels that have ever actually changed those attitudes. Even there, it could be argued that change was coming anyway, as attested by increasing Northern exasperation with the South in the 1850s and by the civil rights movement and some positive responses to it in the early 1960s.

This paragraph and the subsequent paragraphs outline the counter-argument – that fiction surely does not change attitudes.

In this paragraph, as in the others, there is frequent repetition of the keywords in the question, e.g. 'change', 'perceptions'. This is a reminder to the examiner that the essay is maintaining focus.

This essay takes the line that even though a book might be mentioned in the syllabus, it does not necessarily mean that everyone has to agree that the book shaped/changed/reflected perceptions.

The conclusion refers back to the argument set out in the introduction. It would have been better if it were longer, but it does introduce a persuasive new point.

This is a reasonably good essay. It covers a range of issues and supports its arguments with appropriate knowledge. The argument is sustained throughout the essay and the focus rarely falters. It is a shame that there is not more on the side of the argument that fiction *has* changed perceptions, but the possibility that it has is explored sometimes. The conclusion is rather hurried.

What would the examiner think?

Look at the mark scheme on page 104–5. Note the requirements for Level 5 and use four different colours to annotate where you can see the requirements in the bullet points in the mark scheme being demonstrated in this essay.

Glossary

Affirmative action Help for those who have had a disadvantageous start in life, also known as 'positive discrimination'.

Amendment Under the Constitution, Congress could add amendments (changes or new points) to the Constitution. Amendments needed ratification (approval) by 75 per cent of the states.

Black Panthers A black organisation (1966–82) that did some useful community work (e.g., education, provision of food), but aroused white hostility by challenging police brutality. That led to the police, FBI and Nixon administration targeting the Black Panthers, which, in combination with internal divisions and criminal activities, led to the group's decline in the 1970s.

Black Power movement Black Power is a controversial term with different meanings such as black pride, black economic self-sufficiency, black violence, black separatism, black nationalism, black political power, black working-class revolution and black domination. The Black Power 'movement' was never coordinated. It peaked in the late 1960s and early 1970s.

Civil rights These include having the vote in free elections, equal treatment under the law, equal opportunities in areas such as education and work, and freedom of speech, religion and movement.

Congress The US equivalent to Britain's Parliament, consisting of the Senate and the House of Representatives. Voters in each American state elect two senators to sit in the Senate and several congressmen (the number depends on the size of the state's population) to sit in the House of Representatives.

Constitution The rules and system by which a country's government works. The USA has a written constitution.

Congress of Racial Equality (CORE) A black civil rights organisation set up in the 1940s with mostly student members. CORE played an important role in the sit-ins and the Freedom Rides, but grew disillusioned with the slow rate of progress and became more militant for a brief period in the late 1960s.

Democrats Members of the Democratic Party, which dominated US politics in the first half of the nineteenth century. It was pro-slavery and against a powerful central/federal government. It changed during the twentieth century, becoming the party of the less privileged and advocating federal government aid for them.

Depression When a country's economy is struggling. Prices and wages fall, and many people are unemployed, as in the USA after 1929.

Federal government The USA, as a federation of many separate states (e.g. South Carolina, New York), has a federal government. The federal government consists of the president, Congress and the Supreme Court. The states have many powers reserved to them by the Constitution, e.g. voting, education.

Filibuster Procedure whereby the minority party in Congress can slow down proceedings so as to stop legislation being enacted.

Freedom Rides In 1961, civil rights activists, mostly members of CORE and SNCC, travelled across the South on interstate buses to demonstrate that Supreme Court rulings against segregation in interstate transportation were being ignored. The consequent publicity encouraged Attorney General Robert Kennedy to try to enforce the rulings.

Jim Crow laws Segregationist practices enforceable by law, introduced in the Southern states in the late nineteenth century.

National Association for the Advancement of Colored People (NAACP) Long-lasting and effective organisation established in the early twentieth century to promote greater black equality.

National Guard State-based US Armed Forces reserves.

Nation of Islam A black nationalist/separatist religious group, set up in 1930.

New Deal President Franklin Roosevelt's programme to bring the USA out of the economic depression.

Post-racial A society that has gone beyond racism and discrimination.

Projects Federal government housing subsidised for low income citizens.

Reconstruction The process of rebuilding and reforming the 11 ex–Confederate states and restoring them to the Union. Reconstruction occurred in two main stages: Presidential Reconstruction, then Congressional or Radical Reconstruction.

Republicans Members of the anti-slavery Republican Party which emerged in the 1850s. Radical Republicans were particularly anti-slavery.

Rust Belt The old, declining industrial areas of the United States, e.g. the steel towns of Pennsylvania.

Shantytown Rough area with poorly constructed dwellings.

Sit-ins These were protests against segregated facilities. They did not get much publicity until the sit-ins in 1960 in Greensboro, North Carolina, stimulated sit-ins across the South. Many of the black students involved belonged to CORE, while SNCC developed from the sit-ins of 1960. These protests led to the desegregation of many eating places.

State legislatures Each state had its own version of the US Congress, which passed laws relating to the particular state.

Student Non-Violent Coordinating Committee (SNCC) Student activist organisation established after the sit-ins of 1960. SNCC students participated in the Freedom Rides in 1961, but preferred to work at grassroots level, where their most notable achievement was promoting black voter registration in the Mississippi Delta. Disillusioned by the lack of federal protection during their Mississippi Freedom Summer (1964), which aimed at the political liberation of the local black population, the SNCC became more radical. The radicalism increased under the leadership of Stokely Carmichael (from 1966). After an abortive amalgamation with the Black Panthers, the SNCC quickly sank into irrelevance.

Supreme Court The judicial branch of the US federal government. The highest court in the land, it rules (adjudges) whether actions are in line with the American Constitution and the law.

White flight After the Second World War, increasing numbers of whites left large cities in order to escape high taxes, congestion, pollution and minorities. These whites migrated to the mushrooming suburbs.

Key figures

Stokely Carmichael (1941–98) Born in the West Indies, he attended Howard University. He participated in CORE's Freedom Rides in 1961, and in 1964 he worked for the SNCC in Mississippi. He was deeply disillusioned when a Democrat National Convention would not allow any black representatives of Mississippi to participate fully in the convention. He became the SNCC's leader in 1966 and gained national fame with a speech advocating Black Power on the Meredith March (1966). Some members grew tired of 'Starmichael's' celebrity status and he soon gave up the leadership. He gravitated toward the Black Panthers, but in 1969 left the United States to live in Africa with his African wife.

Bull Connor (1897–1973) An Alabama-born politician, he was Commissioner of Public Safety for Alabama's largest city, Birmingham, in the years 1936–54 and 1957–63. A conservative Southern Democrat, he was a staunch opponent of the civil rights movement. In 1961, he allowed the Ku Klux Klan to attack Freedom Riders in Birmingham. In 1963, his treatment of black protesters during SCLC's Birmingham campaign gained the civil rights movement favourable publicity and probably assisted the passage of the 1964 Civil Rights Act.

W.E.B. Du Bois (1868–1963) Born in Massachusetts, he attended an integrated high school. He attended the black Fisk University in Tennessee, then studied at Harvard and in Europe. He taught in several Northern universities, then became a professor at the University of Atlanta in Georgia. In 1903, he wrote *The Souls of Black Folk*, which identified the 'color line' as the greatest problem of the century. In 1909, he was important in the establishment of the NAACP and he edited its magazine *The Crisis* from 1909–34. During the Cold War, he became increasingly anti-American and emigrated to Africa.

Dwight D. Eisenhower (1890–1969) A career soldier, General Eisenhower commanded the victorious Allied forces in Europe in the Second World War, which led to his election to the presidency (1953–1961). He improved America's roads and balanced the federal budget, but had little sympathy for the civil rights movement. He extracted the United States from the Korean War, but greatly increased US involvement in Vietnam.

Marcus Garvey (1887–1940) Born in Jamaica, he established the Universal Negro Improvement Association (UNIA) in 1914, then moved from Jamaica to Harlem in 1916. He created the first black mass movement in the USA, emphasising racial pride, self-respect and self-reliance. He was deported in 1927.

Ulysses S. Grant (1822–85) was a career soldier who played a very important part in the North's victory in the American Civil War (1861–65). He was unusually sympathetic to black Americans during Reconstruction while commanding general of the United States Army (1864–69) and then as president (1869–77). He has long been considered an ineffective president, due to corruption scandals, but recent historians have tried to rehabilitate him.

Andrew Johnson (1808–75) was born in North Carolina. A tailor by trade, he entered Tennessee politics and held several offices, including US senator. A Democrat, he served as Lincoln's vice president in 1865 and became president upon Lincoln's assassination. He frequently clashed with the Republican-dominated Congress, which considered him too sympathetic to Southern whites and nearly impeached him. His presidency is generally considered unsuccessful.

Lyndon Johnson (1908–73) Texas-born Johnson worked as a teacher, congressional aide, New Deal official, congressman, senator (1949–61) and then as Kennedy's vice president (1961–63). He became president after Kennedy's assassination, and was then elected in his own right in 1964. His aim as president was a 'Great Society', in which America would be free of poverty and racism, but he was forced to focus increasingly on the Vietnam War, which made him very unpopular. He was an exceptionally helpful president to black Americans.

John F. Kennedy (1917–63) Born into a wealthy, ambitious Irish-American family in Boston, his heroism in the Second World War helped his election to the US House of Representatives (1947–53), the US Senate (1953–60) and to the presidency. As president (1961–63), his greatest preoccupation was the Cold War. He was increasingly helpful to black Americans before his assassination in November 1963.

Martin Luther King Jr (1929–68) Born into a middle-class family of ministers in Georgia, King was the leading spokesman for black Americans in the years 1956–65. He contributed to the Montgomery Bus Boycott. His 'I have a dream' speech was the highlight of the March on Washington (1963). His Birmingham campaign (1963) contributed to the passage of the Civil Rights Act (1964), and his Selma campaign was vital to the passage of the Voting Rights Act (1965). He was less successful in combating ghetto problems. His 'dream' was integrationist, so he was greatly criticised by black separatists. He was assassinated by a white racist.

Abraham Lincoln (1809–65) Lincoln was a backwoodsman who became a lawyer then a politician. His opposition to the expansion of slavery led the South to secede from the Union when he was elected president in 1860. As president, he masterminded the North's defeat of the South. During his presidency (1861–65), he grew increasingly sympathetic to black slaves, whose emancipation he ensured. He was assassinated by a Confederate sympathiser, and is generally ranked as one of the greatest American presidents.

Malcom X (1925–65) Like his Garvey-ite father, Malcolm supported separatism and nationalism. He joined the Nation of Islam while in prison and recruited thousands of members to that church during the 1950s. White Americans considered his 'by any means necessary' philosophy dangerous. He mocked Martin Luther King's non-violence and inspired a new and more militant generation of black leaders such as SNCC's Stokely Carmichael, along with the Black Power movement.

Thurgood Marshall (1908–93) Born in Baltimore, which he said was as segregated as any Southern city, he was not allowed to enter the University of Maryland, so he attended all-black Howard University. In 1935, the NAACP employed him as a lawyer, and he won many great NAACP legal victories against segregated schools and lower-paid black teachers in Maryland and Virginia (1935–40), segregated universities (e.g. Sweatt v. Painter 1950), and segregated schools (Brown v. Board of Education, 1954). President Kennedy promoted him to the US Court of Appeals in New York, and in 1967 President Johnson made him the first black Supreme Court justice.

Barack Obama (1961–) Born in Hawaii to an absentee African father and a white mother, he lived with his mother and her second husband in Indonesia in 1967–71. After that, he lived with his grandparents in Hawaii and won a scholarship to an elite private school. From 1985, he worked as a community organiser in Chicago, then attended Harvard Law School in 1988–91. He was the first black editor of the *Harvard Law Review*, so a publishing company commissioned him to write his autobiography, *Dreams From My Father* (1995). After Harvard, he returned to Chicago, where he worked for a small law firm that helped black Americans and on a black voter drive. In 1996, he was elected to the Illinois Senate, where some black senators called him a 'white man in black face'. After eight years in the Illinois Senate, he was elected to the US Senate. He was one of the few senators to speak against the war in Iraq. He gained further national attention in a speech entitled *'The Audacity of Hope'* at the 2004 Democrat National Convention. His second book, *The Audacity of Hope* (2006), further publicised his carefully crafted narrative as someone who represented the triumph of the American Dream and hope for change. He was elected president in 2008, then again in 2012.

Rosa Parks (1913–2005) Alabama-born Rosa Parks was an NAACP activist who came to prominence when she agreed to be NAACP's test case in the fight against segregated bus practices in Montgomery, Alabama. Her arrest for refusing to give up her seat to a white passenger triggered the Montgomery bus boycott and, many think, the whole civil rights movement. She subsequently moved to Detroit, where she continued her activism.

Sidney Poitier (1927–) Born when his Bahamian parents were visiting Miami, he grew up in the Bahamas, but moved to New York aged 16. He took menial jobs, then joined the North American Negro Theatre. After some Broadway success, he focused on movies. He was the first black male actor to be nominated for (1958) and to win (1963) an Academy Award. He was the first black superstar actor – and the only one for many years. He felt he was the 'token black', while other black Americans felt his characters were emasculated. He said he would have preferred to have been defined by his acting ability rather than his colour.

A. Philip Randolph (1890–1979) Born in Florida, he was politicised in New York City, where he edited a radical black magazine during the First World War. He was asked to organise black railroad porters, and in 1925 set up the Brotherhood of Sleeping Car Porters union, which gave him great influence amongst black activists. His threatened March on Washington DC in protest against discrimination in the defence industry led President Roosevelt to establish the Fair Employment Practices Commission. In 1948, he used the Cold War situation to pressurise President Truman into desegregating the military. In 1963, he masterminded and dominated the March on Washington, which probably helped the passage of the 1964 Civil Rights Act.

Eleanor Roosevelt (1884–1962) Born into the New York elite, she married her cousin Franklin Roosevelt. She encouraged him to remain in politics after he contracted polio and was an unprecedentedly active First Lady (1933–45). She was 'the eyes and ears' of President Roosevelt's New Deal and worked particularly hard to promote equality of opportunity for black Americans.

Franklin Roosevelt (1882–1945) Born into an elite New York family, Roosevelt had a successful political career (despite contracting polio in 1921) before his election as president. As president (1933–45), his initial preoccupation was his New Deal, which helped sustain Americans during the Great Depression. During 1941–45, his preoccupation was winning the war against Germany and Japan. He is generally considered one of America's greatest presidents. He was unusually sympathetic to black Americans.

Harriet Beecher Stowe (1811–96) Born into a deeply religious and well-educated family in Connecticut, she met and married academic and abolitionist Calvin Ellis Stowe when the family moved to Cincinnati, Ohio. The couple frequently sheltered escaped slaves and in 1851–52, her 40-instalment *Uncle Tom's Cabin* was published in the anti-slavery newspaper *The National Era*. It was then published in novel form in 1852. It subsequently went through countless editions and is considered one of the most influential books ever written.

Earl Warren (1891–1974) A lawyer by training, he was the Republican governor of California for three consecutive terms (1943–53). His 10 years in office were characterised by his progressivism. He was chief justice of the US Supreme Court from 1953–69, and is best remembered for his role in the seminal Brown v. Board of Education ruling (1954). He surprised everyone with his liberalism while chief justice.

Timeline

1852	Publication of *Uncle Tom's Cabin*
1861–65	American Civil War
1862	September – Emancipation Proclamation announced
1863	January – Emancipation Proclamation issued
1865	April – Civil War ended; President Lincoln assassinated; Andrew Johnson became president
	April – December: Presidential Reconstruction
1866	Civil Rights Act
	Ku Klux Klan established
1867	Congressional Reconstruction began, e.g. Military Reconstruction Act
1868	14th Amendment (black Americans granted citizenship)
1870	15th Amendment (black American males enfranchised)
	Force Acts gave President Grant powers to crush the Klan
1872	Amnesty Act helped restore political power to former Confederates
1875	Civil Rights Act tried to prevent discrimination in public places
1877	Withdrawal of federal troops from the South ended Reconstruction; Jim Crow era began
1879	20,000 black 'Exodusters' migrated to Kansas
1883	Civil Rights Cases
1885	*Adventures of Huckleberry Finn* published
1887	Florida rail travel change
1890	Mississippi introduced income and literacy qualifications to stop black voting
1896	Plessy v. Ferguson
1898	Williams v. Mississippi
	Louisiana's grandfather clause
1899	Cumming v. Board of Education
1900	Serious race riots in New York City
1905	Mass migration into Harlem began
1909	NAACP established
1915	Box office triumph of *Birth of a Nation*
1919	Race riots in Chicago and 24 other American cities
1920s	Harlem Renaissance
1920	Cotton prices slumped
1921	Black community destroyed in Tulsa, Oklahoma

1925	A. Philip Randolph established labour union for railroad porters
	UNIA membership peaked
1929	Wall Street crash triggered the Great Depression
1933	March – Roosevelt became president and initiated New Deal programmes; Civilian Conservation Corps (CCC) established
	May – Agricultural Adjustment Administration (AAA), Federal Emergency Relief Administration (FERA) and Tennessee Valley Authority (TVA) established
	June – National Recovery Administration (NRA) and Public Works administration (PWA) established
1934	June – Federal Housing Administration (FHA) established
	Costigan-Wagner anti-lynching bill defeated
1935	March – Harlem race riots
	April – Works Progress Administration (WPA) established
	July – Wagner Act
	August – Social Security Act
1936	*Gone With the Wind* published (filmed 1939)
1941	June – Fair Employment Practices Commission established
	December – Japanese attacked Pearl Harbor
1943	Significant race riots in Detroit and Harlem
1945	Second World War ended
1947	Construction of first Levittown began
1948	Supreme Court ruling against restrictive covenants (generally ignored)
1949	Congressional urban renewal programme
1950s	Malcom X successfully recruiting for Nation of Islam
1951	Housing riots in Cicero, Chicago
1954	Brown v. Board of Education ruling
1956	Montgomery bus boycott
1957	King established SCLC
1960	SNCC established after sit-ins
	To Kill a Mockingbird published (filmed 1962)
1961	Freedom Rides
1963	Summer – SCLC Birmingham campaign; March on Washington; Kennedy promoted civil rights bill
	November – Johnson became president
1964–68	Annual ghetto riots
1964	SNCC's Mississippi Freedom Summer
	Civil Rights Act

1965	January–February – King's Selma campaign	1968	April – King assassinated; Fair Housing Act
	August – Voting Rights Act; Watts riots	1977	*Roots* televised
1966	King's Chicago campaign	1987	*Beloved* published (filmed 1998)
	July – Meredith March; CORE and SNCC increasingly advocated Black Power	1988	*Mississippi Burning*
		1992	*Malcolm X*
	October – Black Panthers established	2002–08	*The Wire*
1967	July – Newark riots	2009	*The Help* published (filmed 2011)
	Guess Who's Coming to Dinner		

Mark schemes

For some of the activities in the book it will be useful to refer to the mark scheme. Paper 3 requires two mark schemes, one for the AO1 assessments in Section B and C, and another for Section A's AO2 assessment.

AO1 mark scheme

- **Analytical focus**
- **Accurate detail**
- **Supported judgement**
- Argument and structure

AS		A-level
1–4	Level 1 • **Simplistic, limited focus** • **Limited detail, limited accuracy** • **No judgement or asserted judgement** • Limited organisation, no argument	1–3
5–10	Level 2 • **Descriptive, implicit focus** • **Limited detail, mostly accurate** • **Judgement with limited support** • Basic organisation, limited argument	4–7
11–16	Level 3 • **Some analysis, clear focus (may be descriptive in places)** • **Some detail, mostly accurate** • **Judgement with some support, based on implicit criteria** • Some organisation, the argument is broadly clear	8–12
17–20	Level 4 • **Clear analysis, clear focus (may be uneven)** • **Sufficient detail, mostly accurate** • **Judgement with some support, based on valid criteria** • Generally well-organised, logical argument (may lack precision)	13–16
	Level 5 • **Sustained analysis, clear focus** • **Sufficient accurate detail, fully answers the question** • **Judgement with full support, based on valid criteria (considers relative significance)** • Well-organised, logical argument communicated with precision	17–20

Quick quizzes at **www.hoddereducation.co.uk/myrevisionnotes**

AO2 mark scheme

Level	Marks	Description
1	1–3	• Surface-level comprehension of the Source, demonstrated by quoting or paraphrasing, without analysis. • Some relevant knowledge of the historical context is included, but links to the Source are limited. • Either no overall evaluation of the Source, or discussion of reliability and utility is very basic.
2	4–7	• Some understanding of the Source, demonstrated by selecting and summarising relevant information. • Some relevant knowledge of the historical context is added to the Source to support or challenge the detail it includes. • An overall judgement is presented, but with limited support. Discussion of reliability and utility are based on a limited discussion of provenance and may reflect invalid assumptions.
3	8–12	• Understanding of the Source, demonstrated by some analysis of key points, explaining their meaning and valid inferences. • Relevant knowledge of the historical context is used to support inferences. Contextual knowledge is also used to expand on, support or challenge matters of detail from the Source. • An overall judgement is presented, which relates to the nature and purpose of the Source. The judgement is based on valid criteria, but the support is likely to be limited.
4	13–16	• Analysis of the Source, demonstrated by examining the evidence to make reasoned inferences. Valid distinctions are made between information and opinion. Treatment of the two enquiries may be uneven. • Relevant knowledge of the historical context is used to reveal and discuss the limitations of Source's content. The answer attempts to interpret the Source material in the context of the values and assumptions of the society it comes from. • Evaluation of the Sources reflects how much weight the evidence of the Sources can bear. Evaluation is based on valid criteria. Aspects of the judgement may have limited support.
5	17–20	• Confident interrogation of the Source, in relation to both enquiries, demonstrated by reasoned inferences. The answer shows a range of ways the Source can be used, making valid distinctions between information and opinion. • Relevant knowledge of the historical context is used to reveal and discuss the limitations of Sources' content. The answer interprets the Source material in the context of the values and assumptions of the society it comes from. • Evaluation of the Source reflects how much weight the evidence of the Source can bear and may distinguish between the degrees to which aspects of the Sources can be useful. Evaluation is based on valid criteria.

Answers

Key topic 1: 'Free at last', 1865–77

Page 7, Spot the mistake

The third sentence in the paragraph is irrelevant. The paragraph would benefit from making the sentence at the end refer back to the question, e.g.: 'Although the war had not been fought to end slavery, by the end of the war, the North's determination to end …'

Support or challenge?

Statements 1, 3 and 4 challenge.

Statements 2 and 5 support.

Page 9, Eliminate irrelevance

The 'poverty and tailor' and the 'people elected in 1865' sentences are irrelevant to the question of his sympathy.

Complete the paragraph

'Overall, Frederick Douglass was correct in asserting that the work had only just begun.'

Page 11, Write the question

Assess the value of the source for revealing the impact of emancipation upon the slaves and white American attitudes to the freed slaves.

Page 13, Simple essay style

1   Black voting led to the election of black officials (700,000 black voters were registered; there were 16 black congressmen and two black senators in the US Congress; over 1,000 blacks were elected to local positions such as sheriff).

2   Black legislators contributed to the passage of laws (over 700 served in state legislatures; they voted for increased expenditure on education; they voted for equal access to public facilities such as railroads).

3   Too few blacks were elected (the proportion of black officials was way below the proportion of the Southern black population; no Southern state Senate had a black majority, with the exception of 65 per cent black South Carolina; black Americans were rarely elected to statewide office – there were only two black senators in the US Congress and there was no black state governor).

4   Black Southerners lacked political experience (Southern black leaders recognised their inexperience and invariably deferred to whites; slaves were rarely educated by their masters, who had not allowed them to organise and therefore to gain any semblance of political practice; blacks were in the minority in every state except South Carolina and Mississippi).

Introduction: The 15th Amendment and Congressional Reconstruction gave black Americans some political power in the South for the first time. Black voting led to the election of black officials who helped improve black status. However, black Americans did not gain political equality, because whites continued to dominate the Republican Party in the South and black Americans were inexperienced in politics.

Conclusion: In conclusion, despite the 700,000 registered black voters and the election of well over 1,000 black officials, black Americans failed to achieve political equality. A disproportionate number of whites were elected in the South, and this owed much to the lack of previous black political experience. Even the vote could not guarantee immediate political equality.

Page 15, Complete the paragraph

Overall, the Klan was highly significant in the South in the 1870s.

Support or challenge?

Statements 1 and 4 support.

Statements 2, 3, 5 and 6 challenge.

Page 17, Simple essay style

1   Grant wanted to focus on the North (economic depression from 1873; continuing westward expansion; disliked having to send in federal troops to keep corrupt Republican state government in power in Louisiana).

2   White Northerners increasingly sympathetic to white Southerners (tired of Southern election riots, e.g. Colfax Massacre 1873; Grant's 1872 Amnesty Act; Supreme Court reflected white opinion when it declared the 1875 Civil Rights Act unconstitutional in 1883).

3   Republican president Rutherford B. Hayes was the one who physically ended Reconstruction (disputed election in 1877; keeping federal troops in the South was expensive, especially with westward expansion and Native Americans; Radical Republicans were dying out).

4   Increased Democrat electoral triumphs (took control of US House of Representatives in 1874; 'redeemed' most of the South quite quickly – Tennessee 1869, Virginia and North Carolina in 1870, Georgia 1871, Texas 1873, Arkansas and Alabama 1874, Mississippi and Louisiana 1876, Florida and South Carolina 1877).

Page 23, Write the question

Assess the value of the source for revealing white attitudes to black Americans and the role of the Supreme Court in relation to black Americans in the years 1875–83.

Page 25, Spot the mistake

The second sentence is irrelevant – the specified time for coverage is 'after the Civil War'.

Develop the detail

The spread of the Jim Crow laws owed a great deal to the federal system of government. The American Constitution had reserved great powers over issues such as voting, transportation, education and law enforcement to the individual states. However, it was Southern white racism that was the main reason for the introduction of *de jure* segregation. Once the slaves were freed, whites became very conscious of the issue of blacks and whites in close proximity in public places. The expansion of railroad travel in the 1870s brought the issue to prominence and states began to introduce *de jure* segregation on railroad cars, for example., the Florida state law of 1887. The Jim Crow laws then spread to other areas of Southern life such as education and recreation.

Page 27, Delete as applicable

'White Southerners used several methods to exclude black voters and these were successful to a *great extent*.'

'Clearly, Southern attempts to exclude black voters were *extremely successful* because …'

Page 29, Identify the concept

1 Significance
2 Change/continuity
3 Consequences
4 Cause
5 Similarities/differences

You're the examiner

This would get into Level 5 – 20 marks. It has a clear focus, sustained analysis, a judgement with full supporting substantiation, internal coherence to the paragraph, a logical argument and is communicated with precision.

Page 33, Identify an argument

The second answer contains an argument that relates directly to the question.

Page 35, Simple essay style

1 Lack of black representation (black Americans could vote in the North but white racism ensured no blacks were elected to statewide office; only one black American in the US House of Representatives in the 1930s, representing a Chicago district; black representation in elected offices, nationwide, was disproportionately low).

2 Southern Democrats in US Congress (South a single-party state, so politicians repeatedly re-elected; long-serving Southern Democrats chaired and dominated key committees in US Congress under seniority rules; Southern Democrats could filibuster effectively, e.g. Costigan-Wagner bills in 1934–35).

3 White American racism (discrimination in North demonstrated racism, so Northerners were not going to be much help; *de facto* segregation in North, e.g. Chicago's South Side; Malcolm X's brother said police officers in Michigan as bad as in the South).

4 President Roosevelt's concern about the New Deal to combat the economic depression (prime concern unemployment and helping industry and agriculture; did not want to alienate Southern Democrats as that could stop other essential New Deal legislation; New Deal employment and Social Security measures helped many black Americans).

Turning assertion into argument

1 … anti-lynching legislation would deter Southern whites from using a favourite method of race control.

2 … Southern Democrats in Congress were able to stage filibusters such as the seven-week one that halted the passage of the Costigan-Wagner bill in 1935.

3 … it was headline news across America, unlike most Southern lynchings.

4 … their filibusters killed the Costigan-Wagner anti-lynching bill in 1935.

Page 37, Establish criteria

Definition: most important reason amongst other reasons.

Criteria to judge the extent to which large landowners were primarily responsible for the suffering:
- problems before the Depression
- other reasons during the Depression
- impact of large landowners.

Reach a judgement

Criterion 1 – agricultural overproduction had led to problems such as lower prices *before* the Depression.

Criterion 2 – other reasons for the suffering during the Depression included the AAA, which gave incentives to farmers to decrease production.

Criterion 3 – had a great impact (evictions, kept compensation for themselves, used federal money to mechanise).

Sum up judgement: The basic problem was overproduction – that led to the AAA policies, of which large landowners took advantage. Overproduction was the main problem.

Page 39, Eliminate irrelevance

Irrelevant sentences here are the first sentence and the last but one sentence.

Page 41, Qualify your judgement

Judgement 3 is the best. Any assessment of the usefulness of the source has to cover ways in which the source is both useful and not useful.

Page 43, Delete as applicable

'She contributed *considerably* …'

'She made *a significant contribution* to the idea …'

Identify key phrases

Key phrase content: changing black voting.

Definition of that key phrase: Why did black Americans switch from voting Republican to voting Democrat in the 1930s?

Key phrase evaluation: most important factor.

Key phrase directing you to evaluation: How accurate.

Essay plan: introduction – there are several factors … but the most important factor is …

Paragraph 1: Eleanor Roosevelt's importance.

Paragraph 2: Importance of lack of Republican aid to black Americans.

Paragraph 3: New Deal had some negatives for black Americans but …

Paragraph 4: … it also had some positives.

The second question focuses upon political/economic/social status and what factors (including Eleanor) impacted upon that status.

Page 49, Moving from assertion to argument

1   … by its erosion of Plessy v. Ferguson (1896) in subsequent rulings such as Brown v. Board of Education (1954).

2   … because there was large-scale white resistance that delayed integration, as demonstrated at Little Rock.

3   … because he said appointing him was his 'biggest damn fool mistake'.

4   … because nothing other than the buses was desegregated in Montgomery.

The flaw in the argument

It was the NAACP litigation that ended the segregation.

Page 51, Select the detail

1   Motivated by personal sense of injustice – 'I was being denied an opportunity to go to a school which I was eminently qualified to go to'; 'because I was Jewish'.

2   Religion – 'My involvement came about from my religious conviction.'

3   Decade of protest – 'all the kids being involved in all those kinds of activities, it just snowballed … it was infectious'; 'a snowball effect'; 'I saw the young people in the first sit-ins.'

Page 53, Developing an argument

King's Birmingham campaign in 1963 exposed Southern white racism to the world. The media showed Bull Connor's use of police dogs and fire hoses against black children as young as six years old. Soon after, King's 'I have a dream' speech during the March on Washington inspired many white Americans to live up to their declared ideals and beliefs. He referred to the Declaration of Independence, the Constitution and the Bible. This contributed to the passage of the 1964 Civil Rights Act, although changing white opinion, the desire to pass the assassinated Kennedy's bill and Johnson's hard work were equally if not more important. King had a third great success at Selma in 1965, where his campaign exposed Southern white racism, notably on Bloody Sunday. On this occasion, black activism was the most important factor in the passage of civil rights legislation, because Johnson had been trying but failing to get voting rights legislation past Congress for nearly a year and it took Selma and Bloody Sunday to force them to pass the Voting Rights Act.

Page 55, Simple essay style

1   He worked hard on many individual members of Congress ('Johnson treatment'; 'bribing'; bullying).

2   Other factors in 1964 (black activism, e.g. Birmingham; white opinion changing – 68 per cent favoured bill; Kennedy's assassination).

3   Other factors in 1965 (Selma crucial – Bloody Sunday; press coverage; humiliation in the Cold War – the world's leading democracy).

4   Other factors in 1968 (King's assassination; Johnson's emotive appeals, e.g. emphasised rats killing babies in ghettos).

Introduction: The civil rights legislation of the 1960s owed much to Lyndon Johnson, but as he said, 'The real hero of this struggle is the American Negro.' It is extremely doubtful that white opinion would have changed and Congress would have responded, no matter what Johnson did, had black activism not drawn the nation's attention to Jim Crow, discrimination and white Southern violence.

Conclusion: While Johnson worked hard to get the Civil Rights Acts of 1964 and 1968 and the Voting Rights Act of 1965 through Congress, it is doubtful that he could have done so had it not been for the black achievement in keeping black issues on the national political agenda. This was evident in 1963, when it was Birmingham that made Kennedy promote the civil rights bill with greater enthusiasm, and in 1965, when Johnson's efforts to get Congress to pass voting rights legislation proved of no avail until Bloody Sunday shamed Southern racists.

Support or challenge?

Statements 1, 2, 3 and 6 support.

Statements 4 and 5 challenge.

Page 57, Spot the mistake

The paragraph describes Malcolm's importance rather than focusing on whether his was a positive role.

Page 63, Support your judgement

1   … because Hillary Clinton's campaign failed to create a similar community that repeatedly donated, frequently volunteered and was inspired to register to vote.

2   … , whereas Clinton seemed stale in comparison, having been around for a long time as First Lady and a US senator.

Page 65, Spot the inference

Statements:

1 – I, 2 – S, 3 – S, 4 – X, 5 – I, 6 – P.

Page 71, Complete the paragraph

Overall, this migration exported Southern race problems across the nation, and this transference constituted the most important turning point in the changing geographical distribution of black Americans in the years 1850–2009.

Eliminate irrelevance

Delete the 'Southern white fears' sentence.

Page 73, Developing an argument

Around 1.6 million black Southerners migrated North between 1910 and 1930, and most of those did so during the First World War. Northern employers actively recruited black workers because the war cut off their supply of East European immigrant labour. Pay was better in the North and black Americans already resident there told Southern friends and relations that life improved without Jim Crow and with the ability to vote. The Great Migration probably constituted the most significant redistribution of America's black population and as the First World War years were the earliest and most significant years of the first Great Migration, it can be persuasively argued that the First World War was the key turning point in the changing geographical distribution of black Americans in the period 1850–2009.

Page 77, Complete the paragraph

So, while migration improved the lives of black Americans in many ways, white violence and racism were problems not confined to the South.

You're the examiner

This gets into Level 2 – 7 marks. This is 'descriptive' with only an 'implicit focus' on the question, even though the candidate obviously knows the material.

Page 79, Turning assertion into argument

1   … because some black Southerners migrated North or West.

2   … in that they stoned the black youth who accidentally strayed into the 'white' part of the Chicago beach.

3   … because black Tulsans armed themselves as soon as rumours of the supposed assault were heard.

4   … in the Watts riots in 1965, $40 million worth of damage was done and mostly white businesses were targeted.

Page 81, The flaw in the argument

Black Americans were in the ghettos because of the Great Migration rather than because of the creation of suburbs.

Page 85, Delete as applicable

'… but as Harriet Beecher Stowe proved, they could be *very influential*.'

'… this was surely a reflection of *a great change* in the …'

Turning assertion into argument

1   … attitudes to race changed, for example, the use of the word 'nigger' became politically incorrect.

2   … *Adventures of Huckleberry Finn* became a standard on the American school curriculum and was therefore read over a far longer period of time.

Page 87, You're the examiner

This gets into Level 5 – 20 marks. It has a clear focus on and sustained analysis of perceptions and sufficient accurate detail.

Page 89, Establish criteria

Definition: Fictional black characters reflect white perceptions.

Criterion 1: Evidence that they have reflected some/many perceptions.

Criterion 2: Evidence that they have not reflected some/many perceptions.

Page 91, Complete the paragraph

Contemporary portrayals certainly reflected common white perceptions of black Americans, and no doubt sometimes helped shape them.

Page 95, Support or challenge?

It could be said that 1, 2 and 4 are arguable and only 3 challenges.

The flaw in the argument

Just because people watched and liked a TV series about nineteenth-century black lives does not mean that it changed their perceptions of twentieth-century black lives. Most whites had long ago accepted that slavery was 'bad'.